For the many good friends who suffered in tough jobs, under bad managers, whose experience I draw from to write this book. Even to those whose bad manager was this author.

© West Michigan Signature Publishing, LLC

ISBN-10: 1453712364

ISBN-13: 9781453712368

Table of Career Paths

Get a job with:

Campaigns - offer your skills, work extremely hard

-Many can get some kind of campaign job for some compensation, but few excel at upward advancement. What sets them apart? I talk about it in chapter six. Which books will help get you in the right mindset? We cover those in the appendix and summarize them throughout.

Political Organizations - start at the bottom, move up fast

-Everyone has advice and an opinion about how to get a plum job working for state party, but unless your parents are major donors or you have dirt on the governor, it can be hard to get it. This book covers the nuts and bolts of how to get jobs when you only have you, your record, and your hard work to get ahead, from researching the job, getting the offer, excelling at the job, transferring to another position, and even knowing the right time to leave the field. This book will also offer you a trick during your offer letter negotiations to get an instant raise and start your job with respect instead of being seen as a pack mule for 'gofer' tasks.

Nonprofits - start volunteering there, help raise money, and be invaluable

-Don't miss our section on seeing the full range of politics, chapter 1, there are great opportunities you might never consider in your area.

-The advice at the end of chapter three, about where not to work and how to diagnose that early, will save you years of frustration and give you the work satisfaction you deserve.

Government - find someone you know on the inside, get any position, and make lateral moves

-Contrary to popular belief, people can get fired from government jobs, and chapter seven will give you great ways to avoid that fate.

-The advice in chapter six about avoiding power struggles will help you, especially in a very political office, survive a manager's transition or keep working even when a new political regime comes to town.

Media - start writing clips and getting them noticed

-You know to build a portfolio and make friends with reporters, but do you know what kind of writing most interest groups need, and how that differs from the kind of writing you'll want to use for campaigns? Your writing samples to a campaign might be communicating the exact wrong style of writing and you don't even know it. Chapter four covers this by talking about the types of writing most employers are looking for.

Major donors - get a skill set and demonstrate it well, make a wealthy friend, and make them want to have you on staff

> -Most never consider working for a major donor, or the local political player, but they can provide some of the best and most reliable political jobs with the least hassles, with good pay and the flexibility to do great things.

I. Table of Contents

Chapter 1 -	Seeing the Full Range of Politics	11
Chapter 2 -	Before Getting the Job	23
Chapter 3 -	Deciding What Kind of Job You Want	27
Chapter 4 -	Getting the Job	45
Chapter 5 -	Keeping the Job	63
Chapter 6 -	Doing Well at the Job	78
Chapter 7 -	Getting Fired and Bouncing Back	112
Chapter 8 -	Finding Better Jobs and Getting Promoted	120
Chapter 9 -	Leaving the Job, Getting a New Job	124
Chapter 10 -	Leaving Politics/Changing Your Role	127

Appendices

A.	Political Terms	131
B.	Great Books Relevant to Politics	132
C.	Political Technology Training Outfits	133
D.	Types of Jobs	134
E.	Potential Starting Points	136
F.	Finding a Job Electronically	138
G.	Typical Political Positions and Titles	139
H.	Budgets and Staff Sizes of Various Campaigns and Nonprofits	140
I.	Interview Questions You Should be Ready for	142
j.	How Most People Spend Their Time and Why They Get Fired	144
k.	Ten Skills Needed in Politics and Ten Great Ways to be a Great Employee	145
l.	Assessing a Race and a Community, What You Can Do	146
m.	Major Politicos and How They Got Their Start	148

Acknowledgements

I'd like to thank Jason Miller and Jeffrey Holst for approaching me about this book, this topic and idea, and entrusting me with it, their patience, and encouraging me to finish it.

I'd like to thank a few special people who have helped me survive several tough jobs, through their patience, understanding and care. Those people are Brooke, Iris, Joanie and Chanel.

Politically, I'd like to thank Wayne Williams for waging a losing candidacy for the Kansas State Senate that led me into applied politics. Wayne was a great man whose heart was pure and despite every setback, I keep hoping to find someone like him to work for again.

In the workplace, I am forever indebted to Jim Eltringham, Josh, John Paul DeGance, Jon Burns, Randy Wood, James O'Keefe, Christine DeGregorio, Deb Green, Dan Flynn, Sr. Mary Frances Taymans, Vic Melfa, Ray Ruddy, Anne Fox, Helen Cross, and of course, perhaps most of all, the Honorable Stephen J. Stockman.

During the editing process the input and advice of Bridget Fay, Marty Andrade, Rich Danker, and many others went wonderfully, and their input helped to transform my messy prose and atrocious grammar into something readable. Whatever writing talent I have is all the result of great teachers such as Michael Roberts and Julie Seeley. All mistakes are my own, and their help in minimizing them is greatly appreciated.

II. Introduction

I can't explain my attraction to politics. Some people have it in their families; some people have it in their lives; I had it in my blood. My friends were never interested in the same way and my family sure doesn't understand it, and I suspect you're the same: you've always loved and had a passion for politics. It's always interesting, always changing, and the stakes could not be higher. It's a great time to be interested in politics. It's truly the question of who rules, one answered historically around the world at the end of a gun barrel, but in America every two years at the ballot box.

Politics is a drug, and can be quite an addiction. And if you're addicted, I can only hope that it's for good reasons and to accomplish good things. Plenty are involved just for themselves, or for their own narrow self-interest, and those people are a bore and a chore to be around. That said, to those who don't understand or have that addiction, they just don't get it and perhaps never will. Their connections to politics are the silly Hollywood movies that always focus on the White House. Your interest is policy, campaigns, and local politics that is miles removed from those popular portrayals. The few times you get a glimmer into a campaign, it's always focused on the things that don't really matter or are glamorous and unrealistic depictions of what politics is about and what campaigns are like.

The largest disconnect is the relationship between interest groups and elections, and how all of those things relate to policy. I challenge you to find the movie that showcases running a non-profit.

Perhaps there's no way to capture the pressure, stress, drama, anxiety, joy, and excitement when you have so much invested. When you get more involved, it gets a lot more fun. This sounds bad, but there's also nothing better than watching your opponents go down in flames, savoring each moment of their electoral demise when they are rejected by the voters. Politics is part spectator sport, relishing one's victories and even the defeats of our opponents.

Politics, the decision of who rules, can produce a great amount of good. Whether someone gets a job, whether a small business can hire new workers due to regulations or tax rates, whether a homeless shelter gets its funding and appropriations next year, or whether a new road is built making the single working mother's daily commute 10 minutes instead of 60, are all issues greatly impacted by politics.

You've also been fortunate to get involved at one of the most interesting times in American history, the stakes are high and the pressure is intense. Get ready.

And as you start out, you'll hear scores of bad advice, such as that you should "study" politics in college. This is bad advice. Most political science courses are completely inapplicable to real electoral politics. Government theory courses are interesting, but also largely inapplicable other than understanding the philosophical basis upon which a policy is formed, mostly of interest solely to philosophy professors.

The media is another topic of discussion, something everyone loves to opine about. But its impact is largely overrated when it comes to electoral politics. Controlling it or even guiding it in the day and age of largely democratized media outlets is also a fool's errand. Besides, most of what one needs to know about the media can be learned in a weekend. Spending hours, weeks, and months planning, plotting, and learning about the media is a waste of time. It's just not that complicated.

For many, "success in politics" means just having a job. Aim higher. Make your ambition more than just a paycheck. Be involved to do great things, and keep your idealism today alive; don't let the cynics kill it. You might be shocked to discover how many people are involved but lack the passion, whose excitement has long faded. Don't let their malaise become your own.

These are people who want to read blogs and have an opinion for a living, this is not what politics is, but it's oddly what it's becoming, and you should do something about this. Be the change, be the one taking action. Remembering those good things that we can do with politics, and those people we can help, politics should be used to take important good actions, and you can help people in politics if you keep focused on it.

Never forget that politics is fundamentally about who rules, who gets to use the state and its authority and power. Put another way, it is who gets what, when, where, and how. Laws, rules, and regulations limit that power, but that's what politics is about: who gets to use the government.

People confuse the meaning of the activity all the time, most often to say that it's about "helping people," and I hope that you do help people, but that's just one way to use that power.

Another thing you don't hear often enough, is how few campaigns are actually competitive. This has great implications for you as one seeking a job in politics. Almost 98 percent of all campaigns aren't competitive, meaning that the victor is all but assured before anything happens. House races are gerrymandered so that only about 30 out of 435 seats are really in play, and in the Senate there are only 33 races each cycle, and perhaps only 4-5 are ever really in question. Such is the state of modern politics, and if you want a chance to get a name for yourself, and make a difference, you need to be near one of those races. Your local races, such as for mayor and city council, are often no more competitive, and often much less, than the national races.

And quite a bit of advice in politics comes from people who run campaigns in noncompetitive areas, or running races that are virtually guaranteed to win. It's the advice of a Democrat running in Massachusetts or a Republican from Alabama: interesting, but not really useful when you're trying to mount an insurgent campaign often against all odds. Quite a few consultant careers were borne out of races that they would have had to forfeit in order to lose.

It's difficult to get advice that transcends localities or those who are from advantaged areas, although knowing how to work in politics across the board, local, state and federal, in campaigns, nonprofits and the media just isn't the kind of experiences most people have. Most people don't leave their home state, so the advice you hear can be selective, outside of their skill set, or subconsciously self-serving and self-validating. Most people can't objectively tell you where the competitive elections are most consistently found because they can't look past their state lines or have never had a reason to do so.

And if you're one who dislikes research, or skips ahead to the end, I'll save you the research and tell you that outside some weird outlier areas, the most consistently "in-play" states are the Rust Belt and Great Lakes states. If you want to be active in politics, go to the Minnesota, Wisconsin, Michigan, Ohio, Pennsylvania area and you'll be guaranteed a variety of competitive elections for the next decade. However, there are competitive races in every state if you look for them, or start them.

In any case, I wrote this book because I've had a unique set of circumstances, as one who was entry-level, mid-management, and senior staff at a variety of places under a variety of circumstances. I have helped a decent number of people get political jobs, and even start their own organizations that have then hired their own people.

And I write this book aimed at the kind of person who is raising themselves up not through nepotism or because you're the child of a major donor or board member somewhere, but through hard work, initiative, and because you want to act on your passions. I'm assuming you're relatively new to politics as a profession, not as an interest, and I want to help you because I've been there, and my advice works.

So if you have a billionaire uncle who can make things happen with a phone call, have him make the call, and don't waste your time with this book. But if you have to climb to the top with your blood, sweat, and tears, and are smart enough to know you need guidance and some idea of the mistakes to avoid and counter-intuitive lessons to learn to rise rapidly, this book is for you.

I'm hoping to take my varied experience with political organizations, internships, and exposure to a wide variety of organizations and collect and present that advice in a useful way to help you get ahead. This book is meant to enable people to be better employees and, ultimately, to be better people. Despite partisan differences and ideological fury, most organizations out there are trying to do good, and so it is my hope that more effective people in these organizations will do more good in the world. I hope that's not too naïve.

The book is written in general for political jobs, but also with several side notes and sections designed for specific outfits and even specific roles like campaign managers. I hope you find it useful. If you follow this advice, I know it'll work.

Ben Wetmore

III. Chapters

Chapter 1. Seeing the Full Range of Politics

Most who follow politics only see 5% of it, and most don't follow politics. It may seem odd to say, but the first thing you should do when looking for a job in politics is to step back for a moment and make sure you understand all the places you can apply your passion. Most people think that it's the president or mayor as your options for political involvement due to the way the media depicts politics, but that's far from true.

Politics affects almost all businesses and non-profits, and virtually every wealthy person in your area has a major interest in politics. You can work almost anywhere and be seriously involved in politics. It also obviously depends on what your real goals are for your involvement. Ask yourself, and write down, whether you're involved in politics to advance your philosophical principles, just to work in politics as a career, or to advance your name and personality.

Each are worthwhile goals, and plenty of people fall into those three categories, and no one will judge you if you just want to feel the public validation of winning an election. I once won a write-in campaign in student government with two votes, one of which was my own, and I felt like I had a public mandate. Politics is fun, but figure out why you're involved and it will help narrow your interests. It goes without saying that you'll need to quickly decide which major political party best represents your beliefs and personal political philosophies.

Let's address each goal individually in terms of the right places for you to look. If you're involved with politics primarily to advance your principles, perhaps you want to pass Social Security reform or you really hate the idea of a ballistic missile shield or you have some other esoteric policy proposal you want enacted. Consider focusing your interests on interest groups first and foremost. These groups are the real places where persuading, marketing, and projecting ideas are found. If you love being a policy wonk and love talking about issues, go where the issues are and focus on interest groups.

As a second best place, consider the media. The media gives you access to the public and the ability to subtly shape opinion in your reporting. The media is the best and most powerful interest group around. It's often called the "fourth estate" for good reason, in that it's almost a separate branch of government. It's easy, when you're starting out in politics, to wildly underestimate the power of the media. That industry is in financial turmoil, salaries in the profession were never great, and the work is hard and long, but you get to wield tremendous influence. In many ways, the media is all that the people know, and the corollary to that is that whatever the media doesn't report, doesn't exist. That's a considerable amount of power and clout.

Campaigns are the third best outlet if you care about issues, and the reason it's third is because while it really does affect eventual policy and decisions, very often the "winnable" races are those run by moderate establishment types. It's frustrating and a bit sad how the popular candidates never take sides even on basic issues. You could have a policy polling at 98 percent and a candidate and his consultants will be worrying about alienating the 2 percent that remain. Campaigns are important, campaigns matter a great deal, but if you care about issues, campaigns can be a way to burn out fast.

If your goal is different than working mainly on your principles and is, instead, just a generalized passion for politics, I'd say the easiest and simplest job to pursue would be one in government. And by "government" I mean a very broad cross-section of paychecks written by the local, state, or federal government. You can be a staff member or staff assistant (which are both terms for office staff for an elected official) and be working full-time in politics. Government jobs are safe, relatively available, and allow you to act on what you want.

The second best job for someone who just wants a job in politics is in the media, for many of the reasons I mentioned above. The media is the perfect way to gain and have "access" to decision-makers and to make yourself the most relevant. You will meet everyone in a short period of time, learn how to write well, and everyone will seek you out; the media can be a great stepping stone later.

<u>Where You Can Apply Your Interest in Politics</u>
Principles: interest groups, media, campaigns
Career: government, media, campaigns
You: campaigns, prestigious positions, positions of opportunity

The world of interest groups and the media are perhaps the most important parts, because they determine new policies, they get to set the agenda, and frankly there are more of these types of positions out there. The nature of modern politics is such that every institution and organization is, to some degree, politicized, and your involvement and savvy political direction as part of that organization can be a strong political job even if you don't see it right now. Fundamental to that understanding is to dispel the myths that surround politics.

Politics is not about good feelings, helping people, or television commercials. It seems like that thanks to the lens of the media, and campaigns seem like they spend all their time refining their television commercials to tune just right into the zeitgeist. Many campaigns don't even run TV ads and, instead, try to reach the "people" and that will be enough to win. They think that the connection of their candidacy with the public at large will give victory because their intentions are pure. Nothing could be farther from the truth. Most campaigns, and most of politics, depend on two things alone: money and votes. Money comes from fundraising and votes come from really good voter lists combined with a lot of hard work in turnout.

These are common terms in politics that, no matter what level or aspect of your involvement, you should immediately familiarize yourself with: fundraising, voter lists, and turnout. Every election fundamentally hinges on those three things. You'll hear local political hacks talk about how some previous candidate "just didn't connect" with voters or that another candidate "was running in a bad cycle" or "couldn't get momentum" among the people ... and as appealing as these answers are, and as half-true as many of them might be, they're fundamentally wrong.

Campaigns live and die by the money they raise, the lists they put together, and the turnout they generate for the election. This is not a book about these topics, but I promise that there are plenty that will deal with them and focus on them. You might be saying that this aspect of politics doesn't interest you, and perhaps it doesn't and won't, but you still have to understand that these are the real factors that matter in politics, and that the messaging of commercials, the precise wording of a direct mail letter, or the nuances of a telephone script pale in comparison to the importance of the money that pays for them, the targeted list they are communicated to, or the apparatus that turns those recipients out to vote.

Now, understanding that concept, let's consider how the various organizations you can work for impact those three things: money, lists, and turnout. The media is obviously the biggest player on the block, able to significantly influence all three. But even organizations that are somewhat under-the-radar in terms of their political involvement can yield disproportionate influence. Churches are often seen as important because of their place within a community as a collection of otherwise random people in one location, concentrated weekly: they have good lists, can control turnout, and their people are already predisposed to giving to good causes.

Local businesses have employees who work with the same group of people for eight or more hours a day, they are making a profit or they wouldn't be in business, they have a huge stake in the development of the local economy, and they interact with ten-fold more people in the community as suppliers and customers. Every aspect of your community and every institution in your area is potentially politically relevant to them.

Don't limit your understanding of politics to the official positions, the media-created concept that it's a presidential campaign or bust. I knew a fellow in college who had latched his political future to former Representative Dick Gephardt, and was sure, positive in fact, that Gephardt was going to win the 2000 Democratic Iowa caucuses and sail to the White House. The fact you might be wondering who Dick Gephardt is should indicate that it didn't work out as planned. When your pride tells you that the only outlet for you in politics is at the highest level, realize that that's a gamble and if you lose, you're starting over at zero.

1. The major types of places to consider

You have a wide variety of good places to consider. The most obvious place to look is a **campaign**, though sometimes it can be hard to start on a new one without experience, which is why a new or **upstart campaign** can be a good starting point even if they're considered "a long shot." There are also a variety of **internships** offered either through a campaign or at a **non-profit** that does politically-related work. You should also consider jobs within the **government** and bureaucracy, as well as with the **legislature,** as a way to activate your passion for politics as a job. There is also the potential to cover all of this, observe it, and write about it within the **media** as a politically-relevant job you should consider. We'll talk about each in more detail.

-Campaigns

-Upstart campaigns

- Internships
- Nonprofits
- Media
- Government
- Legislatures

2. How politics is different than business

One thing that you will hear endlessly is how politics either does work like a business or should work like a business. If you're starting out, especially if you've worked a few jobs, you'll have this as your main reference point, so consider a few major differences to avoid this mistake.

These differences aren't a hard and fast rule, but they exist in every political job to one degree or another.

A hard thing to appreciate is that merit does not mean advancement in politics. This is a very difficult thing for ambitious, motivated people to appreciate at first. You get smacked down time and time again, or passed over for positions that go to the children of donors, and you wonder if it's just this awful place you're working and not another. The truth is that there's always much more work than can ever be done in a political organization, so some people fill certain niches, and management, then, doesn't want to lose them from that niche. If you're familiar with the "Peter Principle" in business, in many ways this is the inverse of that. Rather than promoting capable people to the point where they're out of their element, in politics people get pushed down because they do that job so well that their managers don't want to risk the chance that the job they're doing gets displaced.

It is difficult to get promoted. Several friends of mine and I have felt frustrated watching openings appear at organizations or in campaigns and saying "I'm the best person for this position. Surely this time I'll get noticed" and instead get passed over.

There's a lot of nepotism as well. Since there are so few paid positions and keeping donors happy is always top priority, openings can easily go to friends of management or the picks of donors more than they go to the deserving staffers waiting patiently around them.

In many places, especially upstart campaigns and new non-profits, it will constantly seem like you're in panic mode, reacting and never solving problems farther out. Such is the nature of a trial by fire. A business will have ironed out its internal systems, there will be a normal way one is reimbursed, and there will be stable computers, equipment, and workstations. Every campaign, even re-elections but most especially start-up campaigns, are really a start-up business. Political positions within campaigns can often be entirely helter skelter, unpredictable, and high stress. People from a business background, and especially people who haven't worked for many employers before, can find this unnerving.

I once had a scheduler quit after two weeks, citing burnout. This woman was a self-described "workaholic" and even she couldn't take it. Granted, the campaign we were both working on was extremely tough, but it's not a sport for the weak of heart or those who can't handle everything going wrong at once. People in the business world think they can handle politics, but if you notice almost none of the true upstart campaigns who are underfunded and overperforming are ones done by the typical country club business-types.

Business has many things to teach politics, but it is a mistake and a misperception to say that politics "should run like" a business. Just ask Mitt Romney about his 2008 campaign. If that means it should be more efficient, then sure, but if by that they also expect the days to be eight hours long and cash flows to always be positive, or for people with too much work to get another worker to help shoulder that load, they're working in the wrong field.

3. Common misconceptions

Other than the issues regarding the differences between business and politics mentioned above, there are a variety of small misconceptions that can help assist you in getting started.

For instance, one consideration that many people ask about is whether a political science degree is required, and as a political science major, let me assure you that it is *not*. Political science, and its closely related cousin, "government" or "political theory," is almost entirely inapplicable to the kind of politics you're entering. And, in fact, so many people have a political science background that it's refreshing to have someone with an actual degree that can connect with people outside of the political class.

Having a degree in a hard science can help you connect with certain businesses. Even a theology degree can help you connect with churches, and having special skills, hobbies, and talents can all help you connect with potential major donors. It's a bit too bold to say, but perhaps the most useless degree for politics is a political science degree, because the kind of research and studies that one does to fulfill that degree are almost never the kind that is ever used on a campaign, in government, or in interest groups.

Let me give you an example, most political scientists study the executive, the presidency. Its glitz and glamour are no doubt attractive and compelling. But I will guarantee that 100% of those reading this will not have their first campaign be a serious one for the White House. And, even at that, most political scientists will have nothing but the most mundane observations about campaigning, and will, instead, focus on governing. I once had a political science professor estimate that 85 percent of the profession focused on the Presidency, 12 percent on Congress, and perhaps 3 percent on interest groups. Notice I'm not mentioning any focusing on campaigns. Also know that there are two million nonprofits, and many keep the entire political system in place.

A political science degree is certainly not needed, and lacking one will not be a setback at all. Many politicos, such as Karl Rove, don't have one at all. The main reason to have one is so that people don't look down at you for not having one. And so having an interesting degree is a nice conversation starter, but not necessary.

Another major misconception is that you need family connections to get involved. And while they certainly help, and don't discount that distant cousin who works for someone, ask them for help even if they don't agree with you philosophically. Understand, though, that many people don't have one person in their family who is politically involved. In my family, I don't have a single person who stands out as even particularly politically interested. Despite my statements before about how difficult it is to move forward because of merit, it can be done, and, over time, hard work and endurance does pay off, as with anything.

Family connections can only go so far, anyway. They are perhaps most useful for just getting your foot in the door, which is why you should ask your distant cousins for help, and any other relative. Just a small statement from a friend can make all the difference in the world in getting that internship or that entry-level position. If a good friend asks another good friend to place their friend in the opening, more often than not that will be respected and while that might hurt you when its you being passed over, make it work for you by being the one being chosen. Work your family connections to get ahead, but if you lack them, don't get depressed.

That first foot in the door can be a difficult one, and so another major misconception is that you have to do politics "full-time" to be legitimate. A fellow in Michigan, with whom I'm not on especially good terms, works a job full-time that he doesn't have to show up to, and is thus able to do politics full-time. That's a special situation for him, but few jobs require you to work every moment of the day. You might be able to work out an arrangement with your employer to work late, and take an extra hour for lunch and make that your time for political work.

You can attend functions, help set up rallies, go down to the candidate of your choice and volunteer during that time, all while having a stable, secure job and the ability to say no when you want. You can also use an arrangement like that to start your own campaign, but don't think that because you can't find full-time political work that it pushes you out of politics, far from it. There is always an outlet and a need for your work, it's just sometimes difficult to find it and maximize it. In the appendix you'll find a list of ways to activate a community, and even if you can't find a role anywhere else, this list will get you started no matter what.

Looking around for work you can sometimes overlook certain places because they seem too polished or lacking the need. Other places can seem as though their need is too great. All organizations have a need, some are very bad at dealing with new hires or with volunteers, so if you get a bad vibe or are treated poorly as a volunteer, just leave and find another outlet. When looking around for places to apply and get involved, though, don't focus on what you perceive as their finances or their operations. I've repeatedly been shocked by how polished bankrupt groups are and how messy major organizations are, the old adage to not judge a book by its cover is certainly true. The most important and critical consideration is to find a place that has good people to work around, and who is active on the issues or taking the kind of action you want to work on.

It can be difficult to assess how active a group is, as many hide behind policy papers and press releases in lieu of doing real work. A good rule of thumb when walking around is to ask what their outreach is like. Ask to see their mail room, and ask about their phone bank or automated dialers. Some places outsource their phone operations, so don't be too put off if they say they contract that out to others. But the mailroom is a great indication of the organization. If their mailroom is small and clean, the place is inactive. If their mailroom is large, spacious, and a disaster zone, it's a place you want to work. Mailrooms can't stand being a mess for very long, so that's an indication it's a recent mailing that went out, and inactive groups don't do mailings.

Let me write that more plainly: a messy mailroom means that the group is active. Another indication of an active group is a large stack of what's called "white mail," which is the mail that comes back after a mailing due to bad addresses or because the post office decided they didn't care to deliver mail that day. For a normal mailing of 5,000, there can easily be 10% returning to the office, so a small mailing can mean 500 envelopes are stacked in the office somewhere. Large stacks of recent white mail are an indication it's an active organization, and hence somewhere you want to spend your time and effort.

Every group needs your involvement, though, and each group has a large niche just waiting for you, even if they don't know it. If you're young, I'll tell you that I've never seen a nonprofit organization do effective youth outreach, ever. Almost every nonprofit could use someone who would come in, design an informational brochure about their cause or organization, and either hand-deliver or distribute it to targeted people in the community with a small team of people, i.e., your friends.

That's a universal need, and a skill set that you surely already have. An organization that won't let you do that or gives you any kind of resistance is a good indication that, even if the cause is good, the working environment is bad, so use it as another good test of where to work and how to find a worthwhile place to put your efforts, but don't forget that every place has a need for your work even though they sometimes don't realize it.

Another major misconception is not appreciating your own skill set and specific things you have to offer. This is difficult because it's not necessarily what you enjoy doing. Everyone, though, has some unique skill or talent where they do something or make something much better than others. You might have to ask your friends to get an accurate assessment of this, as you'll be tempted to answer with what you personally enjoy.

Find and identify your talents and skills and find a creative way to use them for a campaign. Even obscure skills can be utilized with the right creative mindset. There are so many ways to make a political impact that your skill has an outlet waiting to be used somewhere.

If you're having difficulty finding a way to use your skill, recall that everything in politics comes down to elections, and every election comes down to money, lists, and turnout. Hopefully that helps you to figure out the way your skill can impact one or more of those areas.

Even with potential outlets, and with skills to use, many people get depressed because they're a liberal in Alabama or a conservative in Massachusetts, they feel that because their party is out of power or because they're in a noncompetitive area, that their talents are best used elsewhere. And while tempting, this is also a misnomer. I think the quote is attributed to multiple people, but the admonition to think globally and act locally is most useful here.

When your party is out of power, it gives you a real chance to develop smaller groups of people and approach institutions for change, rather than worrying about the election cycles. Competitive elections are draining events, and while victories are great and inspiring, you can do the same amount of work and lose everything, so consider the opportunities present when you don't have to worry about elections.

Find someone you agree with half of the way, or even just a little. Find a way to get political experience even though you lack the ideal candidate. The truth is, even if you were a liberal in Massachusetts or a conservative in Alabama, your candidates are never going to neatly line up with your beliefs and convictions. So, know that some compromise will be necessary if you're in this position.

The election doesn't have to be a federal level, either. Most races at the local level are uncontested. Your race can be the perennial long-shot, and you can learn a lot through losing and by running a campaign on zero funds. It forces you to orient yourself around a beat-up laptop running Excel and with door-to-door communications, as well as by pinching every penny. The long-shot campaigns will make you an ideal campaigner down the line.

State legislature races are often surprisingly well-paid and can affect billion dollar budgets. Many state budgets affecting millions of people are passed by one vote, one representative in an election that people too often ignore or forget about. These legislators have staffers and become the farm team for open Congressional seats as well. In some places, such as California, the state senate districts are actually larger than the Congressional ones, you can be representing more people as a state senator than as a congressman.

Student government races at many state colleges have more challengers, more competition, and more voters than many local elections. If you really want to get experience with little consequence, for those of you still in college or planning to go, run a candidate in student government and learn the skills there. Campaigns on the cheap are educational, whereas the ones that are well-funded are often not grassroots, dependent on consultants and media buys, and fundamentally don't teach you anything. Focus on the upstarts and you'll have more fun, anyway.

And even if that still doesn't work out, you can start developing lists and start building a broad political network to enact your agenda. That seems a lot to consider, but I'm not saying you have to be immediately successful. If you're in an area with no one of your philosophical mindset, you have nowhere to go but up. Start the political revolution you desire by figuring out how to get started, and enjoy the fun that the builder has in watching a structure start from nothing.

However you get started, and the basis of your initial involvement, another strong piece of advice that helps is to know that all advice is not equal. Everyone has an opinion about politics because they read the news, and the issues involved lend themselves to everyone having an opinion. Maybe people don't care about international policy towards the Falkland Islands, but they do care about race, immigration, and abortion. With those opinions come thoughts, ideas, and advice coming your way about the "right way" to do things and how politics is really done.

The best rule is to take advice from those who have been repeatedly successful at whatever they're offering. Make people prove their credibility on a topic. The local guy at the bar may have been reading the paper for years, but his advice on how to win elections, when he's never run one himself, isn't useful. I once brought in a former congressman to give advice to a referendum campaign only to have a guy whose only experience was that he had once lost a state senate race start explaining the "real way" to win elections to the congressman.

People don't appreciate how bad their advice is, and it can seriously lead you off-track. You will get plenty of advice from people who have uninformed pedestrian observations. You can learn a lot from this advice, but you can also be lead astray, so check the qualifications of the speaker before you act on any specific political advice.

Another major misconception is that people look at and act upon the data. Very often they don't look at it at all, don't know how to accurately put it together, or choose priorities contrary to the data. Data in a campaign and in politics is never perfect, and you should trust your gut, but the data is still an important tool. If you can get a local voter list, and you're pushing a specific political issue, you should find the part of town that has the most "swing" or moderates on your issue and focus your time on them.

Other people around you can get deluded by crazy thoughts like that you can convert anyone and should start with the hardest to convert. For canvassing and door-knocking purposes people will want to canvass a neighborhood they're familiar with or "because they just know" that that's the "right" neighborhood even though your data is telling you that there aren't enough voters there, and that the spacing of the houses will take the canvassers twice as long as another location. Trust your gut, not the guts of others, and when the data conflicts with your gut, err on the side of your data.

The last misconception I'll discuss here is that people waste a lot of precious time on very subjective topics. People talk about general political ideas and media exponentially more than they need to, as both are often incidental to the success of the campaign. Instead, they need to talk about logistics, turnout, contact and name identification—most elections aren't won through pretty yard signs or great messaging in the paper, but in hard work, door-to-door, and raising enough money to do consistent voter contact and turnout. Actual votes matter much more than the perfectly-tuned message. Take the reigns of a campaign's fundraising and all of the sudden the importance of raising money and funding all the many needy things going on in the campaign come into focus.

There is never enough money. And a wise use of money is in contacting donors to raise more of it. When money's tight you want to contact those donors, often seven times before the election, using mass media so that you can get a lot of them at once. If you get more money than that, you spend it on more communication, not the ancillary special projects that might be of interest to you and me, unfortunately. The time and place for long deliberations on high-priced and high-visibility media buys are usually for large campaigns in a very small window of time, and it's a discussion involving the most senior people on the campaign, usually with specialized media consultants.

Real politics is not like the movies, especially in how its day-to-day affairs are like. When you get involved, you'll soon see that communicating a message about the cause or candidate cheaply, often extremely vague and broad messages about the cause or candidate, is by far the majority of the work undertaken, in addition to the logistics that support that simple mission.

4. Starting out, internships, and getting your foot in the door

Getting in the door comes with its own nuances and complications: seeing the full range of politics, knowing the many potential outlets for your passion for politics, understanding the popular misconceptions and knowing that you have a skill to offer a specific group. Starting out, you can try for a full-time or part-time position, paid or unpaid, as an entry-level staffer or as an intern.

Much conventional wisdom on these issues is misleading. Unpaid positions are often a great way to get in the door, and can be surprisingly competitive. Also, many good places will create a position for you if they see a need for your talents. You have to find and identify the decision-maker and convince them to support you and bringing you onto the team instead of just relying on whoever is accepting your resume as the designated catcher for intern resumes.

We'll cover the process to getting hired later in more detail, but let's consider the major misconceptions about getting started and that critical first foot in the door.

The money is always an important first consideration. There are paid and unpaid positions, and a variety of titles and roles that masquerade as unpaid work such as "fellows" and different flavors of internships. Don't let a college degree, work experience, or other personal pride stand in the way of taking any of these positions.

If this is an organization or team you want to work with, do what it takes to get in the door. Focus hard on finding a paid position, don't work for free as that sends a bad message to the staff that you have a low worth, but do the unpaid work if that's what it takes. Don't think that your commitment and hard work won't get noticed, just be careful that it's not taken for granted. If you do end up doing an unpaid position, do it for a set period of time and don't work a single day past that point without asking for a regular salary.

It's very important to be assertive about these positions.

The general kind of work you can expect will initially seem mind-numbing and grueling. Entry-level work is often the proverbial mailroom of a business. You will stuff envelopes, answer phones, and prepare letters for your superiors to send out. It's difficult to relay that day back to your significant other and feel pride in your work, but suck it up. I knew Capitol Hill interns in college who claimed to be writing speeches for senators and doing substantive casework. The people who claim that are outright liars. Interns and entry-level staff just don't get that kind of work, but know that going in and prepare yourself for it.

The tough work leads to more substantive work later. Voter communication solidifies your base, expands your voter file, makes you more secure, and raises more money. Your political position is entirely dependent upon the depth and breadth of your connection with the public. With that in mind, it can be easier to stuff those envelopes, putting its importance in full context.

If you do this, with a good attitude, the staff will see you as a Godsend. Even the cynical old hands will appreciate your hard work. It can be a constant concern of how the staff sees you and your role, and if you are constantly seen as value-added and low drama, you will be popular indeed.

Another major misconception during the job process is that every position has to be immediately connected to the job you want. If you want a full-time position, you may just need to bide your time until the right position opens up elsewhere, and an internship, temporary part-time, or even full-time position can give you the paycheck needed to wait for that right opening. During the job hunt you feel such incredible pressure to just solve that problem and move on, that you can land at places you don't want to work, you make rash decisions.

Be constantly on the hunt for new positions. An easy way to do this is to be a strong and aggressive networker, which entails having a lot of business cards with your name, phone and email on there as well as some identifying note about yourself. You can get business cards cheaply online, and don't be afraid to get a lot. Put a small stack in your car, a small stack in your suit jacket or business clothes, put a few in your wallet or purse, keep some stashed everywhere so you're never without some when the time arises. You can't network without business cards.

A new job can come from a brand new acquaintance, and many times jobs in politics aren't filled with the perfect person, but with the person who is available right now. Keeping your social network seeded with business cards helps keep you on the job market and on the radar. Just doing this can get you a job offer quickly, the rest of the book is really about getting the right position for you and keeping it.

When you do get an offer, and if you get one right away, even if you feel unsure about a place, or you feel torn between two places, it's acceptable to take a position and see how it goes or take an internship and feel out the place. Your workplace decisions are never final, and an unwritten rule for political positions is that there isn't any serious minimum amount of time required for a position, though it's usually best to work at least a year in any position. The point is, though, that the job hunt is an ongoing process, and a choice to work somewhere is not final or permanent, and the pressure you feel should turn itself to joy at the many great opportunities waiting for you, for the rest of your life in politics.

Don't feel stressed and don't feel as though whatever position you're offered has to be the place you'll be working for the next five years.

ACTION STEPS

    1. Choose a political party

    2. Look around and survey the many places to potentially get a political job

    3. Get some business cards

    4. Weigh the first offer or offers carefully, and consider doing it part-time or as an internship to start while you keep yourself on the job market.

Chapter 2. Before Getting the Job

The best thing you can do, before you send out a single resume or sit for a single interview, is to go through a serious self-examination and write out details about yourself. Figure out what your real skill sets are, and which of your natural talents will be most useful for an organization. You might think that your background in graphic design isn't useful for a campaign, but let me tell you, it's an almost guaranteed selling point.

If you don't know it yourself, though, you won't communicate it, they won't find out about it, and you won't get the position.

The old admonition to "know thyself" is critical. What are your real skills?

There are certain things that you do that aren't skills, as well. "Blogging," for instance, isn't a skill. Writing is a skill, editing is a skill, dealing with the technical details of a website, proven web marketing with tangible results are real skills. Something that everyone does and everyone has a connection to is not a real skill.

Another good example is photography. Everyone takes photographs, and everyone, myself included, thinks, that their photographs are the best ever taken. Photography is definitely a skill, but when it's something that a great number of people do, be careful about overplaying it unless you have a clear record of success with it. This is a longer way of saying that blogging is not a skill set.

There are certain skills that will always look better than others. Certainly, no matter what your position entails, having any sort of background in fundraising is always valuable. If you were in scouts and raised money for a major project, or perhaps you lead a team for community service work in college that raised funds for a project, you might have fundraising skills that you haven't even realized. But outside of fundraising, other valuable skills in the most general sense outside of those needed for the specific position are leadership, initiative and creativity, you want to show that you are the proverbial "go-getter" and won't require constant scrutiny and micromanagement.

Those terms, leadership, initiative, and creativity, are vague terms that get thrown around a lot, but in any position that you end up with, have really good ways in which they are clearly broadcast to the interviewer. Show that aspect of your background, show that you can take a project, get results, and find solutions to problems. The most ideal candidate is one who can handle anything, who is like the A-Team, solving whatever problem comes their way.

The three general skills and relevant results will make you look great, but you also want to winnow down your background to one serious skill that is your most marketable one. You want one thing that really sets you apart from the pack, a skill that isn't just something you're familiar with, but something you're really good at. This is what will set you apart later, and what will get you the job. You want to make the hiring managers decide between plain Jane and fundraising Joe.

You want that one skill to sell to them, don't rely on being a jack of all trades, you really want to be good at one thing. It's easy to think that you want to project greatness in all things, and while there's a certain amount of white lying that goes on in interviews, it's a mistake to be greedy. Be honest with some of your shortcomings, and focus on the areas that you are excellent. Have a skill that you are better at, that is real and measurable, than any other applicant they'll run across, and make sure you know what skill that is and how to sell it in an interview.

That one skill, the one way you stand out for the position, is your best selling point and the way in which you'll stand out from the pack. Each leg of the process, the potential employer is taking a stack of resumes and weeding them out, and then doing interviews and weeding people out.

Know and understand that your job isn't to survive to the end; your job is to stand out from the rest and be the person they want to hire. It's tempting to think that you'll be "solid all around" and be noticed that way, but you won't. You won't get noticed because there are enough professional resume helpers and generators that your resume will look like everyone else's. Also, plenty of people boast and lie in their resumes, inflating past accomplishments, so it's tough for the employer to even know what's legitimate and what's not.

Assuming that your solid background, solid grades, good references, and good writing sample will prevail is a recipe for unemployment. You want to stand out, and selling that one unique skill is what's critical.

You might be worrying that you don't have that skill, but that's where the wide world of political training comes into the picture. Even if you've done recruitment for a fraternity or sorority, you have basic recruitment skills. If you've ever kept the books for a school project, you likely know the basics of accounting to be a local campaign's treasurer. The needed skills aren't that difficult or complex. If you don't have a serious skill to offer, or you have a half-developed one, go for training to refine and develop it, show some initiative. There are a variety of outfits, on both ideological sides, that offer specialized training in all sorts of very valuable skills. There are not only fundraising training sessions, but even very specialized skills classes on specific types of fundraising. Even for sending out large quantities of mail, the post office holds a regular training course in how to interact with the post office in the most efficient ways.

Find what skills will be valuable to a potential employer and develop them, get yourself into a personal culture of self-improvement, being a young dog learning new tricks. Put these unique skills, even the half-developed ones, on your resume, and even if you haven't gone through the training, you can mention to potential employers that you plan on going through it. Again, the key is to show initiative, that you're a problem solver. Instead of screwing up the mail a dozen times in a row before going through a boring class about the post office, you're going through it now to avoid the mistakes.

That's the kind of initiative you want to show, and the kind of thing that sets you apart from the pack.

The training sessions are a good network to get plugged into, and a few good starting points for finding out when those training sessions are going on is to contact your state party's office and ask them for upcoming training, and also ask the ideological statewide groups that are politically-oriented. As well, ask people you know who are involved with these groups as to what kind of skills are really in demand, they'll often be very honest that they really need someone with basic technology skills, or they need someone with basic web skills. Those are the kind of classes you can probably attend at your local community college for $25 and a few weekends worth of time, and be an "expert" in the office.

These are the ways to set yourself apart, to get noticed and get the job.

As well, these training sessions are an insanely-great networking opportunity because there are many people from all over your area that you would be hard-pressed to meet in a similar environment. Most of them will be well-lined up to your philosophical disposition, and they're all looking to expand their political network. Have some cheap business cards made up, hand them out, tell people you're looking for work, and take down their information. After you take down their information, actually contact them. Write down one or a few facts about them on the back of the business card before you put it away, and a day or two later send them a friendly email thanking them for talking to you, and reference what you wrote down.

This sounds amazingly simple, and it is, but no one does it. Even those who don't reply to you will always remember that you emailed them, and when you see them again they'll come up to you much easier, the ice will be completely broken. I've given a lot of workshops and gone to many events, and I do this religiously, and in my experience 85% of people don't even reply to your email, and the 15% that do only offer a small comment back, but 100% remember it later. It's critical to getting started that you meet as many people as possible.

Job prospects often come from the oddest of places, and the people who are a "sure thing" to get you a position always fall through. Keep your network wide, and keep in touch with as many people as possible. Training workshops are the perfect place to do that and meet new people.

You should also network with the speakers. Many of the training sessions are volunteer-staffed by lecturers from the local organizations, typically the kind of mid-level managers who are actually making hiring decisions. So, it's a prime place to find a position, and likely an opening that's unadvertised. Go up to the speakers afterwards, even if you barely paid attention, and genuinely thank them for their time and talent, and try to make small talk. It doesn't have to last long, but if you can make a small positive impression, it will mean quite a bit down the line if you run into them again. The speaker won't remember anything you specifically said, but they'll remember so-and-so, you, as "a good guy" or "a bright gal" and that's the kind of positive association you want.

Don't miss the opportunity to make that small and slight positive impression with 90 seconds of your time after listening to their lecture.

Even the bad seminars can yield a great deal of good. I went to one church's training and educational sessions twice, not because I found the material that interesting, but because I liked the groups the speakers represented. At the first one it was a total bust, but my nonprofit boss at the time was ecstatic that I had went and inadvertently met a contact he had been hoping I'd make, out of the three people there. At the second one, I introduced a then-unemployed friend to another activist who, on the spot, set up a future political deal.

The second seminar's content was good, but it was the five minutes of operational talk after everyone had left, after the two hour event, that mattered. It's the meeting after the meeting that mattered. My friend thought it was a dead-end and almost refused to approach this savvy female political activist afterwards, as her speech wasn't well-fitted to what he wanted to do. What he wasn't seeing and appreciating, of course, is that these events are only about the topic at hand on the surface, even if you're skilled in the area being taught there are valuable contacts to be made, and people who can give you a position, put you in touch with other positions, and radically improve your situation through a simple conversation.

Stay late, it can't hurt. Schedule yourself around being early and staying late, and take advantage of the breaks in time to meet new people and introduce yourself. You want to get yourself noticed. Also, at these events there's often a sign-up for an email newsletter, make sure to sign-up for each one. Even though you'll be getting spam for a decade, you'll also expand your network of information about what's going on, and won't miss future training events like these. Stay in the loop, and take advantage of these opportunities when they come up.

It doesn't happen all the time, but training sessions are the right place to make it happen.

ACTION STEPS

1. Write out a critical examination of your personal skills and make sure to take note of any measurable success you've had using those skills.

2. Write out and identify your best selling point, your best skill.

3. Figure out which skills you want to improve upon.

4. Find training opportunities to attend that improve upon those skills.

5. Network hard at the training events, push out your business cards.

6. Sign up for all political email newsletters.

Chapter 3. Deciding What Kind of Job You Want

When you're getting started, it can seem overwhelming just to winnow down the locations you want to put your resume. You decide you want to work on this policy, that campaign, write for that media outlet, all at once and at the same time. It's difficult to focus one's attention and couple it with your real skills to find the right spot for you, and then to match that work environment to one that will best suit your needs. Over-thinking these things, though, can cause you to repeatedly stop getting started, though, and you need to take action.

As discussed before, you have a skill set. You have things that you are uniquely talented at, those skills are useful somewhere and there are many potential political places to work. Now the challenge is to get specific with your interests and talents to figure out what will work best for you. You really have three things you want to consider and flesh out, your talents and skills, the political policies that matter the most to you, and the organizations that can best use your talents on issues that you care about.

---

90 second primer on **Applied Politics**

Campaigns = money x votes / time

Votes:

To have an effective campaign you need **lists** of people identified for your party, cause, or issue. You get these lists from **vendors**, who will sell them or rent them to you, and can often do the work as well, for a premium. You'll only have a limited amount of time and money to spend, though, and you have to balance high-cost vendors with your own in-house **voter contact** done through **calls, literature drops, flyering, robocalls** and **door knocking** in order to reach 50%+1 of how many expected voters, called "turnout," there will be, your **target vote number**.

Money:

You're probably thinking it'd be nice to have a lot of **money** for your campaign, and you'd be right. But starting from scratch, where can you raise a million dollars, legally? Well, you start with a list of people who are known supporters and donors, they are **prospects** until they actually give money, when they become members of your **house file**. You can use **vendors** to help you prospect, i.e. find new donors, but this is often costly. You can prospect and raise money from your house file over the **phones**, through the **mail,** or over the **web**. Even a small **phone bank** of **volunteers** calling through a prospect or house file list can raise needed cash for your campaign. Be aware of **donation limits**, especially in **federal campaigns**, and keep good **records**.

Voter contact:

Contacting voters is the most basic act in politics, so know the terms. You always want to be aware of your **target vote number**, also known as "how many needed to win." There's always a certain **baseline voting** for your party in that area for any race, so the number "**in play**" is usually surprisingly small. This group, sometimes inaccurately called "**swing voters**" is targeted using **data**, **polls** and "**microtargetting**" to profile what kind of voter the campaign can get the most of, in the shortest period of time. What those votes are like, their **demographics** and **location** in the **district** are key questions. Starting out, local campaigns don't need this level of concern about potential voters, usually just raising the "**name identification**" of the candidate in an area will lead to victory. Most campaigns spend tons of money on **paid media**, meaning **advertising**, and hope for **earned media**, which are **news** and **feature** stories in the **local press** as a way to get free advertising instead.

When voters are contacted, collecting any **data** such as their **issue preferences**, i.e., what they care about, and doing follow-ups with them as appropriate is vital. The key is to give the candidate's position on their issue, and making sure they agree with the candidate on that issue. Studies show, however, that most voters will vote for a candidate just when **pleasantly asked** by someone **directly**.

Meaningless terms get thrown around in politics, like "**grassroots**" and "**activism**" in lieu of specifics. Stand out by always providing specifics, make your campaign and political actions tied to a specific positive result. Many use the term "**astroturfing**" as a way to malign certain actions in politics as stilted or artificial. Focus on actions with a clear result and you'll always be ahead of the pack.

As for the "**campaign plan**," no one reads it, no one follows it. It's useful for **major donors** who ask, though, and for campaign managers to show they know what they're doing. Don't ask to read one, ask the campaign manager what the strategy is for reaching the target voter.

We discussed how to get good at something universally applicable, like fundraising. There are many other useful skills as I've alluded to, but you want to make sure you are objectively and truly good at the talent you are trying to offer a potential employer. I knew a fellow who really wanted to do graphic design, and he bought all the expensive programs, equipment and went to classes, and was still awful. Conversely, I knew a girl who did graphic design fabulously, and should have done it full-time, but was comfortable and secure in the job she had, and wouldn't even bill the people she did design work for; the one without talent was trying to work in the profession and the one who was talented wanted to work elsewhere. Match your real talents with what you're offering, don't pursue something because you find it interesting but your product is still terrible.

Polite society refuses to give people honest feedback and serious critiques. If you're not sure if you're really talented, I have a few suggestions. The first is to ask whether someone off the street would pay you to do the work you're offering. Could you actually earn money doing this skill part-time and from your record? A second way to gauge your talent is to ask strangers their opinion of the work without letting them know that you did it. Ask a friend of a friend if they think this is useful, someone whose opinion won't be clouded by your friendship. The third way that works for things that require subjective critique like art, photography, or design, and is perhaps most painful way, is to submit your work anonymously to the internet and solicit comments. Anonymous message boards will give you a critique quickly, that will be about twice as harsh as needed, but will give you a quick idea if your skill is sellable.

If you have an interest, different than a skill, that you would like to pursue in a position, disclose that at an interview. Mention that you would like to learn more about a skill like video editing or fundraising, and that you'd be willing to go to classes and workshops to learn that skill to make it useful to the organization. Don't lie about your talents, and don't overstate your abilities; be honest and it will pay off.

Determining what kind of political policies you are truly passionate about is another major obstacle to getting a job. If you already consider yourself ideologically "liberal" or "conservative," then you have a good starting point. But those general terms can mean many things, and in some cases very different things. There are anti-tax liberals and pro-choice conservatives, and so you still need to define your own personal philosophy a bit better to help guide you in finding the right job.

Everyone wants to "help people" in the abstract, but there are some pretty serious political disagreements on how to go about doing that. The main ways to help people are a large source of disagreement, as is the consideration of the right role of the government in people's lives on certain issues, and also the role of religion. The same political issues from a century ago are often relevant in different forms today, the debates are different but the overall topics are the same.

One needs to recognize which political party they most identify with. Surely no party perfectly encompasses the beliefs of any one person, but there is certainly one party that more identifies one group than another. Conservatives are typically Republicans and liberals are typically Democrats. Libertarians love to play both sides, but even among libertarians there are ones who are more "traditionalist," meaning more "conservative," and those who are more "libertine" and socially liberal. The parties are really just tools of the political process. The real question, as you likely already know, is what your political philosophy is: primarily whether you are liberal or conservative, and perhaps which subset of those broad generalizations you consider yourself.

---

90 second primer on **Political History**

Within politics there are different **political parties**, but also different overall **philosophies**, sometimes referred to as **ideologies**. Typically when referring to an ideology one is referring to a specific subset within a philosophy. The two main political parties are **Republicans** and **Democrats**, and within those parties are people who consider themselves typically either **philosophically** closer to **liberals** or **conservatives**.

Even within those philosophies, there are ideological subsets. There are **progressive** liberals and there are **social** conservatives and **economic** conservatives. A **populist** is one who appeals to the masses, and they can be found, generally, in both parties and in both philosophies.

Barry Goldwater is seen as the first major conservative Republican to be nominated for President, in 1964. Though Franklin Roosevelt is considered very progressive, **George McGovern**'s 1968 campaign is perhaps the first truly progressive candidate for President. Goldwater was not a social conservative, and McGovern was not a populist. In both parties, anyone who is referred to as a **moderate** is usually also considered to be part of the **party establishment**.

Ronald Reagan ran as a conservative on both social and fiscal issues, while **George Bush Sr.** is considered more of a social liberal. **Bill Clinton** was liberal on social issues, but campaigned as a moderate "**New Democrat**" and on making a "**third way**" by being economically more conservative. **George Bush Jr.** ran as both a social and fiscal conservative, but governed as more of a moderate, especially in the wake of the 9/11 attacks. **Howard Dean**'s primary campaign in 2004 was an important organizing moment for the new left. **Barack Obama** campaigned as a social liberal and economic conservative, but has largely been liberal in both as President.

Conservatives consider Goldwater's nomination in 1964, Reagan's election in 1980, and the Republican takeover of Congress in 1994 to be important. Liberals consider Clinton's election in 1992, re-election in 1996, and Obama's 2008 election to be their watershed moments.

It's generally true that conservatives are Republicans and liberals are Democrats, though in the south there are many conservative Democrats and in the north there are liberal Republicans. In the west, there are many libertarians of both parties. Third parties, such as the **Libertarians** are very focused on being economically conservative; some are localized such as the **Democrat Farmer-Labor Party** in Minnesota, which tends to be liberal and the **Conservative Party** in New York, and the **Constitution Party** is focused on being socially conservative.

Each ideology has its own intellectual magazines and web magazines, and even subsets of magazines. There are very well-written prominent liberal magazines, such as the somewhat moderate <u>Atlantic Monthly</u>, somewhat more liberal <u>The New Republic</u>, which is less liberal than <u>The Nation</u>, which is still yet less liberal than <u>Mother Jones</u>. On the right, there is the somewhat moderate <u>Weekly Standard</u>, with the somewhat more conservative <u>National Review</u>, which is less conservative than <u>The American Conservative</u>. While it's a mistake to assume that politics has only two camps, both on a line of "how liberal" or "how conservative" they are, most people look at it like that and that's the simplest explanation.

When you're starting out, you don't need to know the philosophical differences between vdare.com and alternativeright.com and dailykos.com and firedoglake.com, you just need to generally know which camp you fall into, and also which political party you generally identify with. Once you figure it out, though, you should spend the $19 to subscribe to a few of those magazines and check the websites of your ideology on a regular basis and make sure you're signed up on their email lists, RSS feeds and alerts.

The natural starting point to figure out your own ideology is with your family and friends, do you agree with them politically? If you do, it can help guide you considerably. Perhaps your religious beliefs help guide you, or a particular teacher or professor is someone you trust and share many similar beliefs. Go to these people if you have political questions and ask them about the full-range of political issues. Realistically, there are only about a dozen major political issues that circulate and are ones that you need to find an educated position on. To give you an idea, I'd say these are issues you should find a personal answer to:

- Abortion
- Death Penalty
- Gay Marriage
- Immigration
- Race and Affirmative Action
- Religion and its role with government
- Taxes
- Wars and the military (currently in Iraq and Afghanistan, but in the future possibly other places)

You certainly don't need to be militant on any of these issues to be involved with politics, but you do need to be familiar with the arguments for and against each, and ready to discuss these issues. Don't waste your time becoming a scholar on any of them, but anywhere you work, these issues are likely either to come up, or they are going to assume that you fundamentally agree with their political persuasion to a significant degree. Most places are respectful enough to tolerate dissent on one or two major central issues like these, but won't tolerate a staunch liberal working for a conservative place, or the reverse.

You want to know your own political philosophy to the point where you can identify that one organization or cause would be a good fit for the rest of your beliefs. Groups don't explicitly say this, and it's not broadcast on their website nor will it even come up in the interview, but it will definitely be the subtext. If you're a conservative applying to a liberal organization, either your resume will go straight to the shredder or the issue will come up later. Know who you are and you'll find great comfort in finding a place for philosophically like-minded people. As I said in chapter one, politics is so wide and diverse that there are people who share your principles out there with a job waiting for you.

90 second primer on **Economics**

Economics is a wide and diverse field, with many subsets, competing theories and quality academic debate. This is not meant to substitute for an economics course, but rather, give you a quick glimpse of the type of economics discussions you'll most often run into in political and campaign life, they are large generalizations.

Left: state control and regulation to prevent mistakes, control greed, provide for the less fortunate

Two central thinkers on the economic left are **Paul Krugman** and **John Maynard Keynes**. Sources of economic information on the policies of the left come from think tanks like the **Brookings Institute**.

Left wing policies typically favor the **worker** over the **corporation**, the **union** over **Wall Street profits**. Some call the foreign trade policy "protectionism" when it favors workers over what is called "**free trade**," or a removal of **regulations**, **tariffs,** and **restrictions** between trading countries.

Most on the left favor using government power to stimulate supply and demand, to prevent waste and fraud in the economy as well as to protect workers. There are some on the left, though, considered economic centrists who favor free trade and modify these beliefs, sometimes called the **New Democrats**, **neoliberals**, or "**Third Way**" Democrats.

Right: freedom from control to spur innovation, creativity, and efficiency

Three central thinkers on the economic right are **F.A. Hayek, Ludwig Von Mises,** and **Fredrich Bastiat**. In modern time, there are two primary sources for center-right economic information and thinking, the **Cato Institute**, which is somewhat more socially liberal, and the **Von Mises Institute**, which is somewhat more socially conservative.

Both groups are generally considered **libertarian** in their philosophical disposition, and while there is a **Libertarian Party**, the term generally refers to economic theory and not the political party. The more socially liberal crowd reads **Reason Magazine** and the Von Mises Institute crowd frequents **LewRockwell.com**. There are also some business groups and specific non-profits active on the right, such as the **Koch Foundation** and the **Institute for Humane Studies**.

Most people and groups on the right are pretty consistent with their adherence to a free market, though there are those on the right, such as **Pat Buchanan**, who believe in **protectionism**, using the powers of government to protect industry such as through tariffs and tax policy, to save U.S. industries such as manufacturing.

This is all to say that you have a general philosophical disposition to be aware of when applying. Even more specifically, though, there are likely two or three issues that are of paramount interest to you. In political science these are known as "salient" or "preferred" issues, the kind of things people vote on. Some issues are "popular" in the sense that most people agree with it, but it's a "salient" issue if people are so motivated by it that they disregard all the other issues.

A classic example is the anti-abortion/pro-life crowd, who will vote on that single issue alone, regardless of the other issues. Anti-abortion/pro-life people, then, can be considered as what's called "single issue voters" but more specifically on our point have a "preferred" or "salient" issue above all others. You should identify what yours are, and try to match your skills with your general philosophical disposition, working on one of the issues that matters the most to you, at the right type of organization for you.

The way to do that, to figure out which is the right organization fits you, is tough when you don't know what all is out there. An easy way to get started is to find someone who has the ideal first job, or once had the ideal first job, and try to follow in their footsteps. Don't needlessly reinvent the wheel, and learn from the mistakes of others. There is someone who has worked or is working at a good organization who can give you the inside scoop on how to apply and what the working environment is really like.

This person can be a mentor or just a lunch buddy, but you should solicit all the inside dish on the organization you're pursuing. Find out how they got their position, and what aspect of the job really worked. I once applied to a dream job, having worked with the group in other capacities for a few years, and had the recommendation of the outgoing employee and the superior of the hiring manager. I felt like I was a sure-thing. Just to seal the deal I even made a one-page proposal to discuss when arriving, to show that I was serious about the job, knew it well, and would excel at it.

I wasn't chosen.

A month later, they offered me the job after their first person quit after a few weeks. Even though I was the perfect person for the job, I hadn't quite hit on what the hiring manager wanted, which was someone who came off with a bit more polish and panache. I had fumbled the appearance of the interview, and it cost me the job despite literally everything else in my favor. Later, the hiring manager gave me effusive praise and we had a great working relationship, but it's an illustrative lesson that you want to play to what the decision-maker wants, and not what you think the job needs. If the hiring manager wants a proposal, write one, but if they don't, don't. There's one person who makes the hiring decision, and you need to figure out how to impress them.

I had done the right things in finding out about the job, but I interpreted the results the wrong way. I thought that the strength of my argument would prevail, and I didn't sufficiently put myself in the mindset of the hiring manager. When you talk to people who work there, or used to work there, make sure you're not just hearing what you want to hear, probably that you're perfect for the position, assume that you're not perfect for the position and consider the three biggest and best things you can do to be the best person.

Internalize a culture of self-improvement, you'll be well-served for the rest of your life to constantly work on improving yourself so you might as well start here. Don't let this turn into insecurity, but making sure you are constantly working to improve yourself and critically aware of your own problems will help you minimize those and amplify your strengths.

Be honest about your weaknesses and deficits. It doesn't do you any good to ignore the fact you can't wake up on time, or that you can't iron your clothes correctly. Both things have reasonably simple solutions (go to sleep earlier and at a regular time, and either practice ironing, learn from a relative, or just take the clothes out and hang them up straight from the dryer while they're still hot). Many people will just remain obstinate about their faults, though, and won't make the effort to correct them. Whatever problems you have, they're correctable. This advice works for both personal and professional problems.

It would be too much to ask to plan this out, but it's worth considering that you want to match a job with your strengths and one that ignores your weaknesses. Pursue a job that realistically matches what you are good at and what you'll be able to do well.

You want to completely apply yourself if you really want this one job. Even if you don't get it in the end, make sure to put your best foot forward and put 100 percent into the overall process. There are so many people in the working world, and even in politics, who barely put any effort forward, that to truly apply yourself will make you a very welcome candidate.

Most non-profits, campaigns, media outlets, and political groups are very small and lean places, often barely able to meet payroll; they need top-level performers. There are a few groups, however, that are very well-run and well-financed. Both types have certain trade-offs that you should be aware of, and consider when applying.

We've discussed the general breakdown of the political market several times, but it's worth saying again that you should consider where you're going to best fit. The type of organization often comes with many natural byproducts. To refresh, the general types of political organizations are:

1. Campaigns
2. Nonprofits
3. Media outlets
4. Government
5. Legislative offices
6. Working with major donors

Campaigns are always intense, and very exciting but grueling work. There are always a lot of letter-stuffing and menial tasks that have to get done, and it's not fun, but the result is important. Campaigns combine competitiveness, tight unmovable deadlines, and power. Nixon once said that "losers don't legislate" and that well captures the excitement of a campaign: you have very limited time to make a big impact, but that comes with a great deal of stress and multitasking.

Nonprofits are slower, but often stretch every dollar, and can breed a lot of drama due to entrenched bureaucracies and very narrow missions. Media outlets are usually underfunded as well, due to a decade-long downturn fostered in part by the internet, and so it's very difficult to find paying work in the profession. It's fast-paced as well, though, and the access one gets as a reporter is an addiction in itself. It's exhilarating to be around the power-brokers and to communicate with the entire community as a journalist. Government positions are often boring and bureaucratic, but very reliable and wielding a great deal of power. Legislative offices are direct contact with the community, and slower, though with a touch of drama. Working with major donors often pays well, and gives a great deal of flexibility, but your fortune can turn on a dime if they decide to no longer fund your position or cause.

Each group and type of organization and political outlet comes with consequences and trade-offs, consider where your best outlet is and pursue that course. As for benefits, don't expect any generous benefits package on a campaign or for a non-profit startup, but it usually comes with a government, business, or established non-profit position.

Bigger places will have more resources and real budgets. You won't have to get permission to refill your sticky notes and buy basic office supplies, but you also won't have the freedom to undertake new projects and the same level of authority. Big organizations run like a classic organization, with a hierarchy and a great deal of bureaucracy. Some people can thrive in such an environment, and some people suffocate. Either way, consider it before you even start applying to those kinds of organizations.

> *Big places: more resources, less freedom*
> *Smaller places: less resources, more freedom*
> *All political places: drama*

There's a healthy dose of realism to consider as well. Every political organization has drama. If someone tells you there's no drama, it's either the one place in the world that doesn't, they're not being up-front with you, or they're causing the drama. Conversely, if a place has a bad reputation, that's not a for-sure reason to not apply there, word-of-mouth reputations should be treated with a healthy degree of skepticism. Anyone who gets fired from a position for oversleeping every day for three months never says later that they were fired for being lazy, they make up a reason and rumors spread fast.

Every organization and every vendor, especially, is going to have someone who has bad things to say about that organization. When you meet people from there, whether it's a big place or a small place, always realize that you're getting a very biased sliver of what life is really like there, and that reality can often be quite different from what you've heard. Don't decide to avoid an otherwise good place because of bad word-of-mouth.

But if you have one issue or organization in mind, make sure to talk to plenty of current and former staffers about the topic or organization. You'll quickly hear all of the gossip, drama, and places to avoid that is very valuable information to have early on. Look for things that are consistent, the kind of advice that isn't just one person's sour grapes but is a legitimate criticism of the field, movement, or organization.

Start making a list of places you really like, that match policies you really care about, and are the kind of working environment you think will work.

A good way to do this is to just list them all in a spreadsheet. When it comes to nonprofits, the vast majority of regular political jobs, I would define the size of the organization as either a startup, small, medium, or large. Startups have 1-3 staff, and typically less than a 100k budget. Small groups have 3-5 full-time staff and are 100-500k in annual budget. Medium-sized groups are 5-10 full-time staff and 500k-1 million in annual budget, and large organizations are ones with over 10 staff and over a million in annual budget. You can find the budget information on IRS "990" forms, available for free online at guidestar.org. Also, the website charitynavigator.org helps find out more internal information about nonprofits.

You could roughly define campaigns in the same way, with any federal race inherently being a medium to large operation, a statewide or major state race being in the same league, and state senate and state representative races typically being in the small to medium category and city and local races being in the startup and small category. Even though state representative races are often raising less than $100k, this is just for a comparison purpose. This also isn't an editorial comment on those offices or those races, but just as a means of comparison to budgets, staff, responsibilities, associated drama, and workplace environment.

Campaign jobs are essentially seasonal, with campaigns often not hiring until the summer or spring before the election, so it can be tough to live as a campaign worker, you'll need to find another job to pay your bills in the meantime. That's why the non-profit politicos, who often have that flexibility, are often where the campaign staff works when politics is out of season.

As a means of showing a practical application to this advice, if you are the type of worker who wants to do one thing and do it often and well, working for the larger groups might suit you very well. If you need a lot of creative freedom and a lot of workplace flexibility, consider the smaller groups. The type of organization greatly drives the type of environment that results, and though it may seem like big places have the potential to be creative and free, similar to the reputation of Google, few are like that in practice.

One basic piece of advice for all non-profit jobs is that almost every place will have an official "mission statement" that you should read and consider. Oddly, many employees will never read the mission statement of the place they work, and you will never find a clearer elucidation of what the organization is supposed to be doing. Every group says they follow their mission, but few do, though they all take it seriously. Be familiar with the mission and make sure you understand how your beliefs are consistent with that mission, and how your work and job will be used within that mission.

Ideologically, many places are generally right-wing or generally left-wing, so keep that in mind as well. It's pretty rare for a group to successfully stay as a centrist and not get pulled to one or the other. It's also a misnomer to assume that all churches are Republican or that all unions are Democrat. There are many liberal religious people and many conservative union members, and many individual churches and unions are different from the norm, so while there are generalizations and stereotypes, do your own research and find out what your local organizations are like, and also how politically-polarized they are. Perhaps you would assume they would never hire someone with your ideological beliefs, but in fact they're more moderate and receptive to you.

Know and appreciate the stereotypes since they're often true, but don't let them prevent you from applying. The best way to figure out what a group does, and their ideological disposition, is to read their mission statement. Remember that you don't have to agree 100% with everything, but you will need to substantially agree with most of what they represent, and on all the primary issues, and agree not to work against their interests elsewhere.

Some places don't explicitly say "this is our mission statement" on their website, but you can recognize it as the one sentence or single paragraph that encompasses all that the organization is supposed to do. Let's take a few mission statements as an example and see what they can immediately tell us about the organization involved.

The American Civil Liberties Union (ACLU):

> The ACLU is our nation's guardian of liberty, working daily in courts, legislatures and communities to defend and preserve the individual rights and liberties that the Constitution and laws of the United States guarantee everyone in this country.

Right away, we know that this organization is related to civil rights issues as they impact the court. So if one had little interest in legal issues, or was very passionate about a topic that didn't address specifically legal issues, this might not be the right location for an application.

The Heritage Foundation:

> Founded in 1973, The Heritage Foundation is a research and educational institution—a think tank—whose mission is to formulate and promote conservative public policies based on the principles of free enterprise, limited government, individual freedom, traditional American values, and a strong national defense.

The Heritage Foundation is up-front here in saying that they're a "think tank" and educational in nature. They advance policies but aren't doing work on the ground, per se, or if they do it's a side point to their central mission, as explained here. Therefore, if one were looking for campaigns and elections, or if they wanted to take action on the street on specific issues, this would also be a bad fit. Heritage is kind enough, as well, to explicitly identify their ideological orientation, so if one is very liberal, this is obviously not a good place to apply and would likely be an even worse place to work if you're going to be disagreeing with most people all the time.

The National Rifle Association (NRA):

While widely recognized today as a major political force and as America's foremost defender of Second Amendment rights, the NRA has, since its inception, been the premier firearms education organization in the world. But our successes would not be possible without the tireless efforts and countless hours of service our nearly four million members have given to champion Second Amendment rights and support NRA programs. As former Clinton spokesman George Stephanopoulos said, "Let me make one small vote for the NRA. They're good citizens. They call their Congressmen. They write. They vote. They contribute. And they get what they want over time."

By identifying itself as a "political force" one can easily get the impression right away that this group is very politically active and aggressive. Also, by highlighting their membership, they're clearly focused on their members as well and advancing their interest. You should then ask yourself, am I member, would I want to join this group? If you answer no, then you shouldn't apply. As obvious as that might sound to job applicants, I've seen surprising confusion on this point: if you wouldn't join a group to be a member, don't apply. And if you would join but haven't, have a good excuse for your interview as to why you didn't join. For a group like the NRA, which is specifically advancing gun rights in the public sphere, another natural question would be whether you own any guns. If you don't own any, have never fired one, and are uncomfortable around guns, this would be a bad place to apply.

It's a general rule of thumb that applies well to politics in general, not working for someone you wouldn't vote for, not working for a party you wouldn't join or writing for a magazine you wouldn't read. Make sure your interest in getting a job matches the group's mission, the candidate's record, the party's ideology, and the magazine's outlook before you apply.

American-Israeli Public Affairs Committee (AIPAC):

For more than half a century, the American Israel Public Affairs Committee has worked to help make Israel more secure by ensuring that American support remains strong. From a small pro-Israel public affairs boutique in the 1950s, AIPAC has grown into a 100,000-member national grassroots movement described by *The New York Times* as the most important organization affecting America's relationship with Israel."

The mission statement of AIPAC is somewhat bland as to what their actions are that they use to advance their cause, but they clearly identify that they are a membership organization and that they are obviously Israeli. If you have no interest in foreign affairs, or have no strong feelings about America's relationship with Israel, this mission statement should tell you that this would be a bad place to apply. If you don't know anyone who is a member of the organization, as well, that might be an indication that such a place would be a tough working environment.

Again, you don't have to totally agree with an organization on every issue to work there. You can have minor disagreements, but make sure you know the organizational mission, you understand what they do, and you would join them if they had members and agree with them on the fundamental issues.

Organizations want to hire people like them to do specific tasks. They typically don't want to take risks. As a job-hunter, you're looking for a paycheck and a way to work within your passion. You have to take the time to consider how to best match up the relationship between ideology and your skill though. You don't want to waste your time applying to places that don't want you, or if you were hired there that you would be a bad match and only work there a short time.

Even if you already have a job, reassessing your beliefs and the best type of organization for you can help you find the right place for your skills, and to advance your principles. Of the other types of organizations other than non-profits, businesses are typically selling some specific product and campaigns are solely focused on elections. The mission statement for every campaign is quite simple, and the same no matter which office you're running for: identify voters, raise money, and turn out voters, all before the deadline.

In any case, no matter what appeals to you, make sure the organization you're applying to matches what you really want to do. Or if you're forced to take a position that doesn't match up well, that you know what the group is about and that, moving forward, you either find a place that works better for you and transfer, or learn to love the mission in the place you end up.

---

90 second primer on **Interest Groups/Nonprofits**

The term "**interest group**" is widely applied to a variety of what are also sometimes called "**pressure groups**" or "**interests**" in an area. These can be **businesses**, **churches**, **social organizations**, **membership groups**, **unions**, **trade associations**, and more. Some of these are **businesses**, some are **nonprofits**. There are more than two million **nonprofits** alone in the country.

The influence these groups wield is often determined by either the **size of their membership**, their ability to collect and **coordinate campaign donations**, or some special trait of their members.

Some of these groups have **paid members**, who are considered their **annual membership**. People typically join these groups for either **material** reasons, **solidarity,** or **purposive** reasons. The closest attachment is to the groups with material benefits to membership. Auto repair groups, like AAA, are an example of a **material benefits** membership group. Unions are motivated by the camaraderie of fellow workers, **solidarity reasons**, and the material benefits they receive. People join **purposive** groups, such as ones that advocate for lower taxes for everyone, a classic "**free rider**" problem in economics, where all benefit from the work of a few because those members agree with the purpose. **Purposive groups** have the hardest time recruiting members, because people are just signing up for an idea.

> These groups and people who join them have issue preferences and passion on some issues, while other issues are just generally popular. An issue that has **passion** and is preferred by people, meaning they put it in their most important issues, are those that are **voting issues**. Few people vote solely on gun control, but many vote solely for gun rights and join the NRA. These are people who are "**single-issue**" voters, though in practice it is often two or three issues.
>
> The benefit and influence of interest groups in elections is their ability to corral their particular **voting bloc**, as well as coordinate their **donations** and **media coverage**. Once in power, as well, interest groups can aid and augment incumbents through campaign **donations** and flattering **press coverage**.

A few ways to identify bad places to work, even if all the other elements are in your favor, can be hard to spot from a distance. A good six-point common reference point to major systemic problems at an organization would be places with (1) high turnover, (2) really young managers, (3) people in management without the right experience, (4) nonprofessional managers, (5) obvious nepotism or lots of family.

5 Potential Major Workplace Problems
1. Abnormally high turnover
2. Young managers
3. Managers without the right experience
4. Nonprofessional or unprofessional managers
5. Obvious nepotism or family enterprises

Places with high turnover are common in political positions, as well as ones with young employees. People have bad workplace ethics coming out of college, they're paid poorly, and overworked. Turnover in such a situation is normal, but there's a normal amount even among young people. While a normal company might be at 5-10% turnover in a year, among younger people the rate could easily be double, up to 25%. Bad organizations, though, will burn through everyone in less than two years. I worked at a place where, after two years, in a department of a dozen staffers, only one person had more experience with me. Everyone had been fired or pushed out. One caveat that one has to learn is how rare it is for people to leave on their own terms. Most people are "fired" by a gentle request for their resignation within a certain time period, or who feel the pressure coming and leave to avoid the drama.

You will certainly come across organizations that are so poorly run that they churn through employees left and right. And that place might pay better and give better perks to work there, because they obviously have to in order to recruit people to work in that kind of environment. The job I had, I really loved, and am glad I worked there, but it was excruciating in other ways. If you see high turnover, realize what it means and what kind of future is in store for you: eventually the bell will toll for thee if you stay there long enough to get fired.

Young managers are good in some ways, often creative and more flexible than older managers, but if you see a pattern of young managers it should send up an instinctive red flag. What you should be wondering is whether this young management is due to a workplace that won't retain good people for very long, or can't pay people well, or is perhaps going through a growth spurt that is uncontrolled and might ultimately come crashing down. While it's fun to work with people who are younger and closer to your age, you won't get the direction and guidance in the kind of quality management you need to become a much better employee.

Think of it like a new teacher in school. They're more hip, they haven't been burnt out or jaded by the system yet, but the old teacher can predict the future like Nostradamus. They can see what's going to happen as it happens, and can tell you exactly what you need to know to ace a test, or how to learn the subject the best. Your boss or manager is a superior, partner, and also a teacher. You want someone experienced as a manager.

A similar and related problem is when the people in management lack the right experience. Even in business, the problem arises where people aren't promoted from within, and, instead "experienced managers" are brought from outside. The logic goes that people are good at being managers, and don't necessarily need to know the mechanics of making whatever widget is being produced. In politics, where so many things are very subjective and yet yield dramatically different results, inexperienced managers can turn into a real headache very quickly.

Take a relatively simple enterprise, like campus organizing. A seasoned campus organizer knows how to approach a college campus and recruit individuals to take some specific political action. But how would a manager, with no practical experience in that field, direct his people to do it? Well, he might direct them to do it the way he knows best, utilizing sales technology such as phone calls and mailings. As a college student, though, you likely know that most students only use cell phones, and that no one reads their mail. There are a hundred little subtleties that make something simple quite complicated.

Even the political technology of sending out direct mail can be thorny. A mailing to 15,000 people, where you're hoping to get a return of 1,500, can be greatly affected by minor word choice and diction within the letter, almost imperceptible to the layman, enough to cause the difference between a profitable mailing, and one that loses a lot of money. As said before, politics is not like business, and the attempts to make it run like one, while in some respects healthy, can also lead to major frustrations. If you see a political organization run by people who don't really know what they're proverbially selling, who don't fully grasp the political actions they're taking or in some cases don't agree with the tactics, strategy or overall political philosophy, you're going to run into trouble when you come on board and try to do what you're supposed to do.

An inexperienced or willfully ignorant boss can be a major roadblock and cause serious headaches. I used the example about campus organizing specifically, because I was once almost fired for heading out to a campus to help a student in need when my boss wanted me to do my campus-focused job from the office. As a technician on the subject matter at hand, I knew I was right, but since he was my manager, he told me to do his way. I could do my job poorly to his specifications, or I could do it well and ignore his commands. I chose the latter, and barely escaped with my job until I was reigned in and dressed down a bit.

A great organization and a great job can completely hinge on the quality of your manager.

This is not to say that the manager in question, who is still a friend, was not a professional. There are plenty who are not professional and won't be the caliber of manager you want to work for, so you should watch out and take note during your visits and interviews to see what kind of person you'll be working under.

Places run by non-professionals are usually easy to spot. Look for a messy desk, disorganization, and unfocused workers. Initially, one might be inclined to say some combination of "well, everyplace has its drawbacks" or that perhaps they're "so busy" that they can't be bothered with little details like a clean desk. And for young people, that might be the case, but for older ones, such as those over 30, there's really no excuse. Notice this and take action to avoid working in such an environment.

The kind of manager who has a messy desk will likely have other problems that you'll have to deal with. They'll be the ones who come in late, have you work on unrelated side projects, and can make the workplace difficult. They'll forget what they assigned to you, and be upset that you aren't productive but won't recall that they gave you too much work to start with. Disorganized bosses are very difficult to work with, and just the social cost of accommodating their disorder is tough. In any environment, you'll have a certain amount of personal hypocrisy to deal with that's natural and normal. People who are a mess are no fun to be around, though, and you want to be attracted to winners.

> "We have a one party government in America: the winners. The winners are divided between Republicans and Democrats." -Kurt Vonnegut

A good pop culture reference here is the infamous scene from the movie "Glengarry Glen Ross" about guys selling real estate. Needing a pep talk, Alec Baldwin comes from downtown to motivate them again, and does so in extremely demeaning terms. It's not that I would recommend you work with someone who is verbally abusive, but in the scene Baldwin is a winner, he is a hard worker and a high performer. That is the kind of person you want to work for and be around. The workers are the ones who get things done, who focus on production and not office politics, and who are real leaders.

Work around someone who succeeds and whose work ethic rubs off on you. You don't have to become a workaholic, but you want to be around winners.

> "…Because only one thing counts in this life. Get them to sign on the line which is dotted." - Alec Baldwin in "Glengarry Glen Ross"

With a lazy manager, if you have to be on-time all the time and they're constantly late, it will get on your nerves. The little things like that will add up fast and promote office politics, taxing the patience of the people around you and those above you. Look for the kind of person who has high standards for themselves and for you, as it will help you a lot in the long run, and the one who is a harder worker with higher standards will also go further in their career, which will help you as well. Work for a winner, and be around people who are going somewhere.

The behavior of people you spend time around will rub off on you at least a little bit, for better or worse.

The fifth thing to look for in identifying a bad place to work is excessive nepotism. You almost always get dragged into their personal lives, and it's very hard to advance without their consent. Entire campaigns can be family affairs, and it becomes very difficult to be a professional when you're up against a family member who has access to your superiors all the time and have years of history behind them. Family businesses and campaigns have lazy kids in no-work jobs, crazy spouses that make major decisions, crazy spouses who revisit every settled argument from the past, demands that you divert business to a cousin or a relative for three times the market cost for half the quality done in twice the time, and more insanity. It's an easy way to identify a place that isn't run professionally to see a lot of family on staff and intimately, almost excessively, involved.

Avoid working for family enterprises if you can help it. Unless you marry into their family, you'll never be sufficiently of their family to advance your career.

One last thing when choosing an employer, something that I've seen come up several times, is the impact on one's career of working for a "politically charged" organization. Specifically, whether working on a hot-button topic like abortion, race, or a similar topic will adversely impact your career.

The short answer is that everything you do has an impact later, but that working and taking a stand on a political topic is not a fatal hiring liability. There are many positive associations that come from it as well. What you do will affect you and affect your future employment, and there's no easy way to avoid that or cover it up. Be proud of your past work. Your writings and news coverage will show up in a simple Google search after all.

I once had a political consultant say that I had a bright future as a campaign manager, but that I had to erase everything from my digital presence because the only way to get future employment was to be a blank slate. Since then, I've had continuous employment, so I think his concerns, though well-founded, are a bit paranoid and presumptuous. People are not afraid of passion, they just want to make sure you can control it and that you can rein it in if needed.

And besides, you shouldn't cover up who you are; you shouldn't hide a strong political opinion as though it were a scandal of some sort. Don't be afraid to take a stand and work on a topic that you care about, but understand that doing so might mean that you have to calmly explain your choices later to a potential employer who disagrees with them. It also might mean you have to suffer a few consequences for your beliefs.

There are really two ways in which it will limit you. The first is that you won't be able to get certain jobs that aren't consistent with the political beliefs. If you are a stringent supporter of abortion rights and spend several years working on that cause, it will likely be quite difficult to sufficiently explain that decision to a hiring manager at a Catholic organization. In that way, it won't let you hide your true beliefs when applying, you won't be able to pose as a liberal if you're really a conservative. You shouldn't be doing that anyway, so the "limitation" of taking a job at a politically-charged organization isn't that meaningful.

How it is truly limiting is that groups, candidates, businesses, and organizations that have no stance on your hot-button issue of choice will be reluctant to hire you, fearing that you are incapable of toning down that message. By the fact they're moderate or unconcerned about your specific issue, they likely don't have a strong opinion on it either way. So, if you want to mitigate or minimize the potential career damage that a controversial job has, just be ready to show and prove that you are able to keep your political beliefs private and confidential while on the job.

As a side note, some positions of relative public exposure will want to avoid the seeming scandal that comes from your notoriety on a topic. Those situations and positions are rare, but it is something that comes up. And when it does come up, frankly, there's nothing you can do to change it. If you lose a potential job, or if you lose an existing job, just move on and find a place where it won't be a problem. A sincere explanation and a pledge to work hard and avoid drama will go a long way for most employers. The main concern that future employers have is whether you can be a good worker with no-drama, and not create fights with customers and co-workers who disagree with you. Exude that, and your other political passions will not be an issue.

ACTION STEPS

    1. Figure out your best skill

    2. Figure out your ideology

    3. Figure out which issues you're most passionate about

    4. Figure out which kind of organization is going to suit you the best

    5. Make a list of organizations that fit your passions and ideology

    6. Talk to people who work there now or in the past, and look out for consistent complaints about the 5 potential major problems

    7. Find someone who has worked your ideal job before, and follow their path

    8. Decide if you want to work somewhere politically-charged

Chapter 4. Getting the Job

After all the preparation and anxiety of getting into politics full-time, we come to the nuts and bolts of getting the job. We'll cover getting your resume ready, networking with people in the right environments, going to the right meetings and conferences, getting an initial interview, navigating that interview, and the follow up that will make you stand out and get the offer. The problem I hope to leave you with is one where you have to weigh offers and your concern is about taking the job that's right for you, and not choosing out of desperation or fear that you're not going to get another chance.

It's a nerve racking thing, and the preparation and self-improvement that you have hopefully gone through up to this point will serve you well. Simply knowing the political terrain, where you want to work, and what skills they need, and matching your own skills to those needs, really puts you miles ahead of the competition. Give yourself a healthy boost of confidence and optimism about your job prospects because so few really internalize these lessons and the things we've already discussed. I'm not preparing you to get just any job, but the right one for you.

The first thing you need to have ready is a good resume. There are scores of websites, relatives with advice on the subject, and opinions on what makes a perfect resume. For most political jobs, you need a very basic one. Keep it to one-page, as you likely already know, and highlight those things that have application to the job at hand. I don't think it's necessary to have a different resume for each position, but I would make at least two versions of a political resume: one that highlights your partisan experience and one that is more suitable for moderates. Not that you want to hide anything, but what you stress can look a lot different in those two environments.

So many resumes come in for potential job openings that when writing yours keep two things in mind: that it needs to be flawless and have at least one thing that really stands out. Any flaw is a reason for a potential employer to throw away your resume. Some of my best employees have been bad spellers, but you'd be surprised at how easy it is to use something so arbitrary and frankly so stupid as spelling mistakes to toss out a resume. An employer is just looking for reasons to whittle down the pool of applicants from 300 to 12, and spelling is an easy way to do that. So work hard to take out any flaws or errors in your resume. Ideally, the one thing that you list on the resume to stand out is the same skill you want to hype in your interview.

Perhaps that's a little bit of experience with fundraising. It could be a decent background with a unique skill. If you've run your own campaign, at whatever level even student government races, find a way to include those. The resume will provide easy talking points in a future interview. You might be thinking that you can just whip up a resume when you find an opportunity, but when you come across an opening, you'll want to act on it so fast that it'll be too frustrating to start a resume from scratch. Keep in mind that many political jobs are filled in a very small window, you'll find out at a reception that someone's hiring the next day, so you want your resume at the ready to email to them that night, right when you get home, so that it's in front of them right away. Politicos have very short attention spans, and you want to react quickly when opportunities arise.

Be sure to put your contact information on your resume and a good email address. If you get an interview, it's likely to be offered over email, so make sure your spam box isn't catching potential interview offers. Also, make sure your email address is plain, just your name and not something awkward or odd. You may have been known as princess4eva@yahoo.com in high school, but it looks awful on a resume. A shocking number of people do this. Have a plain email address, set it up to automatically forward to your princess4eva account if you must.

Put your basic contact information on a set of business cards including just your name, phone, and email, and maybe a small description about yourself. It can be witty, but don't go overboard or make it confusing. You can get cheap business cards at vistaprint.com or even at your local print shop like FedEx Office. The business cards are needed for whenever you meet people later on, you'll want to get their card and give them yours, and email them your resume soon thereafter, but we'll cover that more in a bit. For right now, get the business cards.

The next thing you want to do is to check your Google results. There are services that will claim they can "scrub" your Google results, but they aren't worth it. Just know that anyone interviewing you will Google your name beforehand, and every inference will be negative, as I said before, they're just looking for a reason to weed people out at this stage. Though you can't control your Google results, you can at least be ready to give coherent and credible explanations to what the employer sees. My second Google result for a long time was "AU's Bad Boy, Ben Wetmore, Speaks!", referring to my alma mater and some activities in college. The article was more flattering than the headline, but I still needed to be ready to discuss and explain that Google hit in my interviews.

If you share a name with a porn star, be ready to explain that you're not the same person. If you are the same person, don't use your stage name. You'll also want to check your Facebook, Myspace, and other social networking profiles before you even start applying. The bland services like LinkedIn that give generic employment data is fine, I'm focusing on the ones that are revealing about your personality in a different way. With sites like Facebook and Myspace, nothing on these sites works in your favor, ever. Your best option is to deactivate your profiles before you start applying. The second best option is to set all your privacy settings to the highest level possible. Know that politics is a small world, though, and friends of friends can still show your potential employer what you've been up to. As I say, nothing on these sites help you. You'll either look too wild, too stuck-up, too nerdy, or too anything for the employer. The best option is to deactivate and potentially reactivate later. These sites are a liability because no one takes a positive view of it. The same thing is true of personal websites; they really never go in your favor. You probably think that it seems logical, rational and is a great service to the community to host your own site, but take it down, at least for the interview process.

Don't give them a reason to reject your application; they're just looking for mistakes.

Another potential source of embarrassment is dating websites. This is even worse than social networking sites. Make sure that you don't have a live profile on any dating site when you start interviewing. Imagine sitting across from the table from someone interviewing you, who just read your profile two days ago and remembers all those witty pick-up lines you tried to put on your profile, or that low-cleavage shot from Cancun you added to attract guys. You're just asking for trouble; make sure you delete these profiles. As these are pay sites, and apparently care less about privacy, it can be a bit harder to delete your profile outright. At a minimum, "update" your profile by deleting all photos and making all your personal information non-specific to you. As with any other incriminating websites, take them down before you interview, nothing will add to your value in the interview. They create more excuses to favor the applicant who is more of a blank slate. It isn't fair, it isn't right, but it's the way it is. Remove your online social presence before it removes you from job consideration.

The network of people in politics, and in your area, is very small. The number of people perusing these websites is even smaller. If you were to think about social networks like a series of Venn diagrams (which are the kind with overlapping circles), you'd see that the twenty-somethings who are single and looking for a relationship and are willing to use an online dating service to get it is a small group. When starting out, it's just too easy to poison your chances by coming off the wrong way. You want to get out there to people you know, who know you, and can help you meet the most people in the shortest period of time.

Start with your friends and network with them first. Make sure they all know that you're looking for a job, and what kind of job you want. Anyone you would feel comfortable sending a Christmas card to, someone whom you would catch up with if you saw them randomly at the mall, anyone whom you have more than a passing connection with, works here. Send each of them your resume and tell them if they hear of any opening, to send your resume and let you know. This sounds obnoxious, and it is, but it works. These are people who care about you, know about you, and want to help you out, so ask for their help. Any job lead is a good one, and the leads can be from the least likely sources.

And even if your friends can't find you full-time work, you can often find small-time, part-time contract work this way. Your friends want to help you out after all, and so the scraps of work sometimes leads to bigger and better offers, and gives you the chance to get out and meet a whole new group of people. A friend once saw me on nearly my last dime and told me to call an editor friend and freelance an article, it worked out, gave me a boost of confidence, and though it wasn't a lot of money, it gave me a good writing sample that helped set me apart when I applied elsewhere. Another time, a former employer I wasn't on especially good terms with referred me to a petitioning service in another state where I was able to make a few hundred bucks and meet an entirely new set of people. Another friend, around that same time, tried to set me up as a driver for a day for a state politician. He made it clear that the job was an unstated try-out for a full-time position as a driver. Having a college degree, I felt that was a bit beneath me, but was willing to do it anyway to open up my options. Another friend, who ended up being his driver, rose through the ranks quickly and is now on his senior staff in less than 18 months because he took the scrap work and worked hard.

Political work and campaigns lend themselves to a lot of temporary jobs and multiple jobs, and as hard and as frustrating as they can be to work at the time, they can often lead to bigger and better things.

Many groups on both the right and left have glorified sales, field, or fundraising jobs that are grueling, but have a lot of openings. Taking this tough job and sticking it out can help you prove yourself to others and give you the respect needed to seriously compete down the line, as well as give you a temporary paycheck. Don't be too proud to take a tough job, or a very entry-level job, and really apply yourself to it.

When people know you're looking, don't be afraid to take the small contract jobs that get tossed your way, they can lead to greater things.

This period of job searching can be quite difficult financially and even emotionally. No matter what, though, work hard at projecting your best face. Always seem like a winner. And don't let the defeat get you down so much that it shows. Your fortunes can turn quickly, as with my friend who went from driver to senior staff. He had been laid off and was quite frustrated just a month or two before the driver position opened up. If you seem dour and depressed, though, you won't be an attractive candidate to anyone. Said more bluntly: a loser is a loser.

Every job has merit and inherent dignity, and there are plenty of political jobs that seem like utter pain. Telemarketing comes to mind. But these jobs lead to better opportunities. Even the high-level jobs in politics involve a lot of this grunt work as well. As a campaign volunteer, it's easy to be resentful about the chore of stuffing envelopes, but it's not much more rewarding to recruit those resentful volunteers and turn them out and keep them happy. The reward in politics is not that the work is fun, but that the rewards are large and the victories are sweet. The work itself, though, like all work, is tough and often grueling.

No matter what, keep a good attitude and project positivity.

This will also help you in the long-run because many jobs are promotions from within. You take the small-time gig, you're a volunteer, you're helping out already, and they see your value and don't want you to slip away, so they offer you a full-time position. The danger in hiring someone new is that they're an unknown commodity. With a regular volunteer, intern, or short-term worker, they are a known commodity and much safer to hire. The classic business adage is that they are "value-added" and worth more than they're paid. You want that to describe you, that you are always "value-added" and contributing much more than you cost.

Most openings aren't advertised for primarily two reasons: groups don't want to take risks on new people and they dread the grueling hiring process. Any proverbial "foot in the door" that you can get makes you a known commodity, makes you worth the risk of putting you on payroll. Their concern is that you'll be a lazy staffer, but if you've demonstrated that you bust your hump all the time to work hard, that concern is gone. There are a variety of odd, out-of-the-way-jobs that almost cater to this odd market. Jobs like "research contractor" exist at think tanks and never get well-advertised. You hear about them through word-of-mouth and often from people who have the job currently and are leaving for greener pastures.

You could be down on your luck, depressed about your job prospects, and go to a small networking event with some friends and meet someone like this who is leaving her job tomorrow. She tells you the position is still unfilled, it's loud, and she can't hear your name, but you heard that they're in need of your unique skill set. It's a temporary job, but if you work hard at it, they might have a full-time position opening up in three months. You give her your business card, take hers, and email them that night with your resume.

That's how it happens, and that's how many people get a job in politics.

You can meet these people, and find out about these kinds of openings, by regularly attending political events, functions, and fundraisers. If you're a student, you can often get into these kinds of events for free. There are often training events held for partisan and non-partisan groups in your state as well; those are great functions to meet people at. It's tough to be in the right mindset when you go to these events, but a good rule of thumb is to take out a set number of business cards, and get into enough small-talk conversations to justify getting out that number of business cards. Your goal is to casually meet people at the event, and for people to remember you when they see you next.

This can seem intimidating for people who aren't inherently social. But remember that there are people whose job it is to meet other people, such as field staff for campaigns, recruiters, hiring managers, people in "grassroots" who want to meet you and find out what you're about. Going to these events, you will easily run into the several people who, just like you, are trying to meet everyone there.

These people you meet don't have to become your cheerleaders, or hear about your many struggles and how you overcame them, they just need to remember your face and make a positive association with it.

There are a whole list of do's and don'ts I would helpfully list here, but they can get too long. A few major things, though, would be to avoid any discussion about controversial topics, since you don't know these people yet. Refrain from rehashing the crazy theory about how 9/11 was an inside job, or the zaniest thing Glenn Beck or Keith Olbermann said yesterday. Don't come across as a nut job. Again, the goal is to create positive associations. Also, avoid aggressively pursuing the hot number you just spotted across the room. Not that you can't succeed, but if you're new to the group and you're immediately going carnal, consider how that's going to look. Be professional, be courteous, keep your hormones in check, and remember that your goal is to get positive associations and your business card out to a decent number of people.

New situations like this can take getting used to, and even though I'm giving this advice, I sometimes have trouble following it. But it's always better to have a wider circle of friends and acquaintances, especially when you're looking for a job, than not. Another point of etiquette as well, is that many other people are wise enough about the job search to play this racket to try and make 30 second friends so that they can get an "in" on a future opening. Be classier than that. Really listen to what people are saying, let other people talk. Don't be up front and pushy with the fact that you're looking for work, ideally don't even mention it. Let them bring it up, it's one of the most natural first questions in politics when you meet someone new, "what do you do?" or "who do you work for?" and have a soft, diplomatic answer, just say that you're looking for good opportunities right now, trying to get out there and meet people, and see what's available. Keep it subtle and classy, and avoid the natural tendency to break down in tears at your problems. Remember that these are first impressions and you want to keep it classy and subtle.

It's so easy and natural to come off bad when they find out you're looking for work, it's somewhat embarrassing, they feel like they need to help you, and after all you just met. Just keep it classy and play it off. You're playing for the long haul, but if they offer to help, take their offer and take any part-time work they suggest as well. If they start a conversation about finding work, ask their advice. Everyone loves to give their opinion.

In any political conversation, let the person talk and talk and talk. You'll glean amazing amounts of information about them in a short period of time. People will tell you all their secrets if you let them. You just want enough information to restart a conversation the next time you see them, or have something to reference back to. Perhaps they really like baseball and then you go to a game and can then talk about it. With men especially, sports is by far the best conversation starter and bond. You want to find ways to build a common bond and social connection. Some people will talk forever, so cut people off after 10 minutes or so, just politely say that you need to talk to someone else before they leave, and that you'd like their card. Be generous, be gracious, but don't waste all your time with one person at an event like this.

One great trick I've learned is to keep their business card out after they offer it, and repeatedly look at the name on the card, it'll help you associate the right name to the face later. Also, if you don't put it away immediately, you look better in that you're not just collecting business cards. Also, find a few facts out about them that are unobtrusive and write the facts down on the back of the card. Good information here is the name of a spouse, how many kids they have, what their passion is, and perhaps who their favorite politician is, etc., things that will help jog your memory later.

Most of these events have a relatively stable set of attendees, the same 40-50 who come out to many of these events. Not casting doubt as to their motives, but many of them are single. In Washington, there are different sects like this by religious affiliation, kind of a set of groupies for whatever niche type of event that goes on, and who regularly attend the same half dozen events each year. What's nice about this is that once you get to know a few people in this social set, many of them will help you out, they talk between one another and so you've done well to enter their circle. Practically what this means is that you shouldn't waste your time trying to become friends with the rest of them if you have other potential social circles to break into.

The book *The Tipping Point* by Malcolm Gladwell, while full of much pop-anthropology crap, is useful in that it well defines certain personality types within similar social circles. There are "social connectors" and "mavens" and different types of people. If you go to these political events and are observant, you'll notice the same types. Try to eyeball who is hanging out with whom regularly, and make friends with each social circle, try to float seamlessly between these different groups and don't get pulled into the drama or gossip naturally within each one.

For what it's worth, the book identifies three primary traits that many people share, being either a "maven" who is highly knowledgeable, "salesmen" who are highly charismatic and persuasive, or "social connectors" who are people who know everyone else. And to a degree, these are useful archetypes to understand. The type of people you want to find out about openings and help broadcast you to others are the social connectors. You can find out about the "real" workings of a place and all the gossip from mavens, and the salesmen can pitch you and be an advocate for you when you find an opening. To the extent that these traits exist in people, figure out the right way to take advantage of people's strengths and let them help you get a job.

Finding them at a political conference is tough at first, but gets easy once you can spot the archetypes. And do your best to run in different circles, always spotting the maven who can tell you where the openings are and the right job for you, and the social connectors to meet others. Make sure to be seen a few times at the common events these circles attend and you'll be a known commodity that they want to help find a job.

I'll say it again, make sure to keep your confidence high at these events. Be someone others want to meet and be around. Odd opportunities can come at the weirdest of times. In November 2006, I was let go from a position in a particularly acrimonious way, pure office politics and backhanded actions that, well, really ruined my day. As I was walking home mid-day after the termination hearing, it felt odd to know that I had absolutely no plans for the next day or week. Later that afternoon, on a fluke, I received two calls, one for part-time contract work that paid better than my normal salary, and another call inviting me as a non-profit leader for another group I lead in a political movement to attend a personal meeting with a major Presidential candidate, with a half dozen others for an hour-long meeting in DC the next day. Since I had nothing better to do, I went and had a great time and spoke with other group leaders who gave me the right direction to take the next position.

Your fortune can change in a moment.

Part of the fun of politics is how entirely unexpected it is, it's the same thrill of the unknown as one would find in gambling. When you're attending these events, your anxiety will naturally be high, you'll wonder if this advice is realistic or applicable to your situation, but just remember that endurance pays off, and great opportunities can come simultaneously with great setbacks. Go to as many political conferences as you can because you'll naturally expand your chances of finding these unique opportunities.

It always pays to be seen. You want to look good, have at least one clean professional business outfit, have your business cards ready, have breath mints and backup breath mints, and a good way to arrange your hair in a quick moment. I've listed out what could seem like a lot of needless detail or perhaps a way to be over-prepared, but you should consider it the bare minimum. Plan for being informed about a major political tradeshow this weekend, full of politicians, campaigns that are hiring, nonprofits that need skilled people, a wide variety of people, and ask yourself if you're prepared to go to it right away. As Seneca said, luck just happens to favor the prepared man.

In addition to the generic political conference and trade shows, there are also a variety of political training sessions that are always going on. These training sessions are put on by a variety of entities, usually state political parties, statewide nonprofits, and the like. They bring in experts to train their "activists" in being effective on a given topic. You should attend as many of these as you can, and if money for the registration fee is an issue, I've never known an organization to turn away an activist who was truly needy and eager to learn. You can usually slip in the back and soak up the knowledge with a polite request and sincere need.

You're going to these training sessions in order to learn a new skill, or further hone an existing one. You should even attend the topics you already feel comfortable with. This is to cement your own personal habit of perpetually being in a "culture of self improvement" where you are always refining your skills. The other two reasons you want to attend these functions, though, is that you meet other people in your area and other entry-level staff, but most importantly you meet the speakers who are giving the presentation.

Going up to them afterward shouldn't be intimidating at all. Ask a point of clarification or a follow-up on a specific point they made. If you're more knowledgeable in the subject area, resist the temptation to go up and correct them on the point or to get into an argument posing as a discussion or helpful tip. In fact, never give speakers critiques in person, if you truly feel compelled to do this, do it in a very respectful letter a week later. Ideally don't do it at all, and let them improve themselves. The reason to stay anonymous is that you want this person's help to get you a position elsewhere, and the last thing you want to be seen as is the obnoxious know-it-all. No one ever wants to hire that person or refer that person to a friend's nonprofit.

So with your point of clarification, know just a bit more from the speaker, demonstrate an interest in the topic, and start a small conversation. Thank them for their presentation, and find a good compliment to give them. I once made the mistake of chiding a presenter who came in from out of town to suggest lobbying legislators on controversial topics through phone calls and emails. The only way to lobby on controversial topics is to have influence with donations, lists, voters, and political brute force. I knew the presentation was stupid advice, and I was right, but it was extremely tacky to have made the point at all. Appreciate the effort these people put forward in order to come work with you today, give them a compliment, and start a relationship.

Tell them you're involved with politics, be subtle about your job needs. Explain that you want to add value to yourself and ask them, sincerely, what they think are valuable skills and the right way to get them. Every speaker loves to give advice, and this subtly introduces into their mind that you're looking for a job. You're setting the groundwork for them to ask you if you know so-and-so, and that they have an opening, and that you might be the perfect person to apply. To get a referral from someone you barely know might seem odd, and perhaps it is, but people in politics do it all the time. And that referral, though it's not the same as from someone you've known for years, makes you stand out. If you've applied to that open position, you're likely to get an interview simply out of respect to the person making the referral.

Campaign and political people love doing favors for one another, they love stacking up a little cache of IOU's and good favor with other groups; it's a way for them to build soft political capital. They want to do favors; you just have to give them a reason. The people performing the training at these kinds of events, somewhat surprisingly, are often the real hiring managers at campaigns and firms. It's the perfect place to find a job in a short period of time.

One good example is older "consultants" who often teach at training events. You've probably already noticed that after three weeks working the phones, a campaign intern is talking about opening a consulting firm and being a political professional. The title "consultant" is perhaps as overused as the dreaded title "activist" which is to say that they're practically meaningless. But someone who is identified as a consultant at a training event actually has clients, and pays their bills that way. If they were a campaign manager they would be identified as such, and consultants are in a very unique position in politics, uniquely able to help you.

These people need perfect reputations because they live and die by word of mouth. They're also very isolated because they often have to work at home or in an office all the time to keep up with the mountains of emails and calls they attend to, if they actually make their living that way. This means they don't interact with new people all that often, and they need a steady stream of new talent to help them staff new campaigns or get new projects off the ground. I knew one consultant who said this explicitly: that he hated doing training but it was the only way for him to meet potential people he could place as staffers later.

The people you meet here will be the ones who can hire, refer and place you later.

They're not going to come out and say this, but that's their motive, that's why they're volunteering their time: to meet motivated people like you who are new and hungry for hard work and a position. They want to do favors for others, and have a network into a multitude of campaigns. Existing campaign people might be limited in what they can do for you, and might have internal drama from a nasty primary or just party politics so that they aren't as well-networked and flexible as a consultant. When you're at a political conference, hunt these people down and make sure they get a positive impression of you and they get your business card.

Woody Allen said that 90% of winning is showing up, which is not only true, but also applies to getting a job offer. Perhaps over 90% is just asking, just being there at the right moment.

My first job offer out of college was running a state Senate race in Virginia. The job didn't work out because of some issues on my part, but the only reason I got it was because I was the only one who went up to a D.C. political consultant after a training session. He explicitly asked people to come up to him and give him their information. This fellow didn't remember me, I don't remember being particularly active during his training session, and I doubt I asked any meaningful question. He had a client who needed a campaign manager, though, and the one thing this consultant knew was that I had been motivated enough to go through political training, which was enough.

It might sound crazy, but it can work that easily. Demonstrate eagerness, network, put yourself out there, and you can get a job offer. Running a state senate race is not going to pay great, and it won't launch a personal political career into Congress, but it is the kind of work that gets you into politics. And it all came as a consequence of showing up.

You can also just show up to political organizations and offer to volunteer. You frankly have a lot more latitude coming in as a volunteer than as a paid entry-level staffer, because since they aren't paying you, they can't fire you. The critical thing, however, is to have a skill to offer to them and also be a self-starter. Many people offer to volunteer, and either bristle at the work they're given, never come back, or refuse to learn a new skill so that they can do the other type of work. This probably derives in no small part from a popular misunderstanding about what kind of work most campaigns and non-profits do, and how much basic communication in the form of mail and phones is involved and constantly needed.

Active organizations are doing a tremendous amount of contact to advertise their programs, solicit potential donors, and impact the community in a variety of ways. Some groups outsource a lot of this to a vendor who handles one aspect or several, but every political organization has a continuous need for this kind of work. Quite a few people will come in and try to change the "messaging" or other highly abstract concepts like "branding" in lieu of the real hard work needed. Appreciate that real work, the needed tasks, are all the kind of grueling ones that feel like real work. Sitting around in an office and talking about ideas and "strategizing" is rarely serious work, but it's easy to get deluded into thinking politics is purely a "war of ideas" instead of, more appropriately, it being a war of logistics and actions.

"Amateurs Talk Tactics, Professionals Talk Logistics." -Gen. Omar Bradley

Many organizations and even campaigns don't know how to effectively use volunteers, so you have to be diligent and persistent. Even with a small amount of experience, a good recommendation and a decent campaign can well set you up for positions with your state party and other campaigns. A friend in St. Louis points out that even in a period of high unemployment, he sees quite a few unfilled job openings.

Another option is field work with a national organization, especially if you're younger. Organizations on both the right and the left put people on the ground in targeted states and in specific areas. On the left this is more available, with positions as a union organizer being the classic example. Many prominent politicos started their career as union organizers. On the right, there are a scattering of groups that do some form of field work, which I should disclose is often very tough, grueling, and under-paid. It is a way to get "in" though, and a job when you need one. Some find it tough to translate that experience into a later career in politics, but I'm not entirely sure why that is. Perhaps they get burned out from the tough work involved with field work. I certainly don't want to oversell it, because it's not easy or pleasant, but it's very real and performance based. The people who thrive at it can do very well.

No matter what experience you end up getting initially, realize that everyone you meet, from entry-level to upper-management and everywhere in between, can potentially help you later. They want to help you, because it's beneficial for them to do so. Your previous internships and employers will all help you if they can, because they want to use you as a good applicant to do someone else a favor, and so much of politics depends on reciprocal favors. When I was looking for a job out of college, I had worked an internship two years prior and recall being a very lackluster intern. I could make excuses, but I'll spare you. I was just a sucky intern. When I was job-hunting, I almost felt ashamed to ask these people for help, but I saw a Vice President at another event and he asked me to stop by.

I went, and he spent an hour with me giving me leads and making calls, really going out of his way. He was definitely a nice guy, but he had a solid self-interest here as well. He wanted to help me find a job, but he also wanted to help a manager friend of his find someone they could trust. It was a truly win-win situation. I was so accustomed to being in a competitive environment and feeling like others were always out for the same job or pursuing the same leads, I forgot about those who will help you without charge. Another former internship, where, again, I felt I wasn't a particularly solid intern, offered me a summer job because they knew I was in need. I'm sure they could have found someone else, but I was a known commodity and they wanted to help me out.

Don't forget about your friends, and the many ways they can help you. In most cases, they want to help you, if you'll just ask.

There's a delicate art in asking these people for job help. It's pretty bold and brash just to call up and ask, to the point of being uncouth. Instead, you want to meet these people by asking them out to lunch. Target the b-level people, remembering that the principals and candidates rarely hire the entry-level people, they delegate that to the Vice Presidents and Department heads most often. If your uncle is the CEO or candidate, sure, that will go a long way, but casually knowing some of those people is often insufficient to get the job. Many people have no hiring authority whatsoever.

The pundits in politics are a good example. You might think that they're extremely well connected or able to command respect through their widely syndicated columns, but they're often entirely powerless to get someone hired. I was at a baseball game once, and this extremely well-connected individual kept telling me how he was going to get me interviews all over town, that "we needed to get me" a position somewhere. He was more enthusiastic than I was. I was really flattered. I could see in his eye, though, that something wasn't quite right. I'll skip to the end of the story and tell you that not a single interview or call came out of it. This fellow was well-connected, he was very bright, and he could no doubt get a job if he needed one, but he had no ability to get one for someone else.

His favors didn't give him the ability to hire others. It's primarily those with their own campaign or nonprofit estates who can curry favor elsewhere, because they have the ability to do a favor in kind. If you run a campaign and can hire someone's friend, then it's expected that later the reverse will be true. Target the people who are the real hiring managers at these groups, not the principals per se, and not the entry level people. It's these mid-level people who are the real people who can help you. The famous writer and columnist, the person you see on TV working individually is often, unfortunately, of little help.

There are plenty of people who will seem as though they're doing you great favors and nothing comes of it, don't get too jaded or resentful about it, many just don't have the authority or the current budgets to make it work. It's largely a quantitative game as well, where you need to talk to as many people as possible to meet a large number. Talk to people in your social circle, the people at your church or in other social settings. Get their feedback, ask for their honest opinion about you as a worker. Everyone likes to give advice. Ask them what worked for them, what they've heard work for others. Don't be pushy, really listen to what they say, and things can soon work out.

When talking to people, make sure you communicate what you're looking for and what skills you bring to the table. As we discussed in previous chapters, having this ready, well understood and easily verbalized will serve you well. You want people to remember that "Jane is looking for an entry-level campaign job and knows computers" in a very simple sense, that's what people are going to take away from your conversation with them and will communicate to the person they know who is hiring. Name plus job type plus skill, that's what you want to leave on the mind of those talking to you.

The major benefit to doing this is that 90% of jobs don't get advertised. People enjoy the doing favors thing for other people more than they enjoy getting whatever wild card applies off the street. I buy all sorts of junk off Craigslist, but if I had a job opening, would I really trust that cornucopia of possibilities, where I'm just as likely to get someone with serious psychological disorders, or trust my colleague to refer the friend he knows? Jobs don't get broadcasted because people want to go with known commodities; they want someone to vouch for the person applying.

The secret is that almost everyone in politics wants to vouch for people they barely know, and will vouch for you if you'll call them for lunch.

The meetings and contacts you talk with should all receive your business card and a prompt follow-up email thanking them for talking with you, and attaching your resume either for them to give you feedback on, or for them to forward on if they hear of any openings. These contacts will lead others to start looking at your resume, and you want to cast as wide a net as possible so keep going to the meetings and events to meet plenty of new people. People will be reviewing your resume, remembering the positive associations they made about you, and putting your information in front of someone able to give you a job.

The resume and personal contacts lead to an interview. Usually the interview is very direct, but sometimes groups or campaigns can be somewhat coy about it all and ask you just to "come in" and get a tour or look around or meet their team. The overall, normal process is that the resume and contacts lead to an interview, which leads to a second interview, which leads to an offer, and then an offer letter, and when you accept and show up on your first day, you've got the job. Understand the process you're starting.

The first interview is absolutely critical. You already know this, but let's recap some basics, like showing up on time. You want to look good, wearing your best professional suit or outfit, arriving early enough to calm your nerves, fix your hair, and check your teeth. Make sure not to have gum when you walk in, and even if it's hot not to be sweating. I once had to run my hands under freezing water for ten minutes to cool down on a hot day during an interview, do whatever it takes.

Crazy things can happen on an interview day. Whatever bad luck karma you're carrying around will all blossom in that very moment. I was applying for a campaign job using a car loaned through a friend, when another friend, convinced that one wouldn't be reliable enough to get to the interview, loaned me his. I left with plenty of time to make it to the interview, which was a decent drive away. I noticed the gas was empty, so I stopped to fill it up, about 30 miles away. The only problem was that the gas tank was locked—with a key that I didn't have.

I called the friend who had loaned me this car, and when he hears my frantic question about where the keys are, he explains that they're unfortunately in his hands. There's no way to make it there and back in time. The friend explains that my only option is to break off the gas lock. I open his trunk to find a five-foot-long crowbar. So there I am, in the freezing cold, with a suit and tie on a highway gas station, using a crowbar designed for a giant, trying to break off a gas cap. I arrived at the meeting location a few minutes late with a cut hand, and my guy was waiting. As I went to shake his hands I had to remember that there was gas all over them and ducked to the bathroom. I left an hour early to be there on time, and was still ten minutes late. You can't possibly get to the interview too early considering the crazy things that will no doubt happen that day.

You want to look good and arrive on time not for its own sake but because the employer is gauging you as a future employee. If you're late, the inference is you're going to be late every day in the future. If you're frumpy and have wrinkled clothes, they're going to know that's what you'll probably be like in the future. Public positions require someone appealing. If you're going to do outreach and work with new people, the organization wants someone appealing, someone attractive, someone who can grab attention. You aren't looking attractive to play on the senses of your interviewers as much as you're demonstrating that you can get people's attention while in the job.

When the interview starts, take notes. Also, be ready to ask a few basic questions about the organization. Everything they say is a clue to how the job will work out. If they say the job has had a lot of turnover, that probably means that you won't be there for long. If they say that they really want a one-year commitment, which is a typical request and general expectation, realize that the job has probably had many people jump ship quickly in the past. No job is perfect, and you get paid to be at work because it can be tough, but the little clues can tell you a lot in an interview setting.

Be perceptive to the things going on in the office, even the pictures, the small comments they make, and the little details. Don't just take a tour and glance, really look at the office and see if you can tell what working there will be like, if you can tell what kind of work they do there, if that place will work for you. I once took a tour of a potential employer, for a receptionist job I didn't get, and they said that there was a lot of chance for upward mobility. I thought that was great, but I looked around and noticed that all the positions above that one had people who had been at the organization for several years, and all had advanced degrees that I lacked. Every place says there's a chance for "upward mobility" because that's what they're supposed to say, and that possibility probably exists in the abstract. But if you can look around and see that it's extremely unlikely, well, ask yourself if being a receptionist is what you want to do for five years waiting for that one opening while you take graduate school classes at night.

They did me a favor by going with someone else.

One question that kills potential applicants in first interviews, which is so easy to answer, is "what do you see yourself doing in five years?" Every interviewer asks this, and every interviewee fumbles the ball here by confessing their own heartfelt desire to do some other job that they're just waiting for, or the job with the CIA that they're hoping to get once their security clearance comes through. People have all sorts of weird plans. The right answer, of course, is that you say you want to be working hard here, part of a strong team, doing well in the department. If you're on a campaign, you should say that you'll be working on the candidate's re-election campaign, or hopefully assisting them in some other way. You want to demonstrate that you plan on joining their team and being loyal to their team. The subtext of this question is to ask if you're committed to the job, not what your secret passions are or what you'd rather be doing. No one wants to hire someone for whom they are the last choice.

So even though you plan on running for Congress in three years, or you have another job opening you're waiting to hear back from, or you're just finishing up your graduate degree over the next year and then you're off to greener pastures, answer as though you're serious about the position and tell them you want to be working there and involved with what they're doing. Frankly, your plans probably won't work out anyway (though you should still have them and work towards them), so give a good solid answer here and don't shoot yourself in the foot. Besides, most places will grow on you over time.

Make a list of interview questions before you arrive and prep good answers to them. Be prepared for basic ones. A classic mistake to make is to be confused about the mission of the organization or the political issues of interest to the candidate. You don't need to go overkill, but be prepared to give smooth answers to basic questions.

Every interviewer will ask you what questions you have. It's better to voice relatively benign ones than actual concerns at this stage. You should voice your material concerns after the job has been offered; you want to negotiate from a position of strength.

Fundamentally, you want to know what you want from the job, but also what they want. Entry-level jobs are usually about the tough work that no one on staff wants to do. Basic campaign jobs involve a lot of mail stuffing, canvassing, calling, and literature drops. There's also sometimes a difference between what they think they want and what they really need. In your mind you might be thinking, "well, they don't know they need my skill but I'm going to revolutionize this place anyway." And you would be very wrong. It's true that campaigns think they want great writers, when in reality they want a sweatshop of people writing at a third-grade reading level. They don't want to read your English literature essay; they want simple press releases and plain-Jane letters to the editor pre-made for supporters.

Almost no place wants real creative writing, serious prose or complex sentences. Rhetorical flourish in politics takes a backseat to the kind of plain-spoken folksy wisdom of people like George Bush, Will Rogers, and Ronald Reagan. As someone who enjoys good writing, I wish it were different, but it isn't. When a place tells you what they want, fit that need, and play to that. If you know deep down that they want something else, or if they are confused about what they want, play to their confusion rather than try to be objectively accurate. Remember that these people with the flawed bias are making the hiring decisions and that if you are absolutely correct but not what they're looking for, they'll choose someone else.

After the first interview, make sure to look over your notes, consider the answers you gave to any questions, and follow up with a handwritten thank-you card and provide any additional information you promised. If you forgot to send a thank you for a week, send it anyway. This is so rare, it's shocking. You can buy a pack of thank-you cards at CVS for $2.50, and there's really no excuse not to send one. A mediocre interview can be saved by a nice thank you note a few days later.

You also want to clear up any confusion or major job requirements in the follow-up note. If your timetables don't work out quite right, that you can't start for two weeks later than they want, it's time to let them know. I lost the campaign manager position out of college due to a car requirement that was disclosed at this point, and it saved us both a lot of extra time and headache, it was just a passing comment where he referred to a car and I was up front that I didn't have one. It's a lot more hassle to deal with these things later.

Make sure to tell them that you'll be following up with them soon, within a week asking them for a decision.

Sometimes you're asked to come to a second interview, usually with a different set of people attending. You want to be ready to say exactly how and why you'll excel at the job. Have a one-page plan that you can share about how you'll hit the ground running. There's a normal 3-4 month transition period for new employees, something every manager dreads. Easing that tension, and that anxiety on their part, by projecting the sense that you are a real "go-getter" will help set you apart. Your boss is concerned about having to train you and the time involved in "getting you up to speed" and the people on your team are worried about you being socially awkward, a jerk, perhaps divisive or just no fun to work with. Play to all their concerns, ease their anxiety.

After a second interview, ask for a date they're going to make their decision and start planning in your head how to leave your current position. Be sure to disclose any potential major problems at this point. I lost a job as a press secretary on a campaign, having had the job for about 12 hours, because the campaign manager overreacted to some political controversies I was involved with in college. I figured it didn't matter, and was all college-focused anyway, so it was unnecessary to disclose. But I was wrong and it was quite relevant. Err on the side of caution and don't surprise your manager with any revelations, keep them in the loop at this point.

Sometimes they'll talk about money at a second interview, sometimes it'll be in the offer letter, and almost always it'll be less than you were expecting. At the second interview, don't do anything passive-aggressive like complain about bills or the high cost of living in the area; don't think that you can plant any seeds that will cause them to offer you more money later, it won't. Even if by some miracle that worked, it would breed a lot of resentment later when they see you buying flashy things. So, don't even talk about money until the offer comes to you.

When they make an offer, you need to have calculated in your head what the minimum you can take the job for, what your minimum livable amount is, and realize that campaigns love to hire people for peanuts, and non-profits aren't much better. You'll have to pay your bills, make ends meet, pay down your credit cards, etc., and you can't be in constant financial distress and be an effective employee. Have a number in mind for what you can afford to work at, realizing that these jobs pay poorly starting out.

This next bit of advice is going to make you thousands of dollars per year over your lifetime, so perk up:

When they make an offer, and this is true for any job, they are always low-balling you. Typically, they are offering you 10 percent less of whatever they were intending to offer you. Let's say the offer is $33,000 a year to make the math simple. For a $33k position, they won't offer you 33, they'll offer 30. Your challenge is to swallow your fear and say that you can't do it for a penny less than 10 percent more than what they have offered, $33,000. There are three potential outcomes here: they match you and say they'll make it work at $33k; they'll say they can't do it at all, money's tight, and 30k is the final offer; or, most likely, they'll say they'll split the difference and give you $32,000. In any case, you're much more likely to make several thousand dollars more per year because you ask for 10 percent more at this moment.

Now, you can't pull this trick more than once, you get one shot at the table here asking for more. You can't argue with whatever number they come back at you with. You have to either accept or refuse their response.

If you are more cavalier about the job, and confident that they really want you, you can hold out for more. I applied for a job where they offered me 30k, and I said I couldn't do it for less than 50k. I was firm and couldn't budge. Financially I was in a tough spot, so this offer was more of a necessity for me at the time. They also knew that a grant I was working off of was drying up soon and thought they could get me cheaply. A week later, they said they could pay me 40k, but that that was the absolute final offer. I told them I couldn't do it for less than 50k, I liked their group a lot, but that was my situation. You want to make sure to be asking for the highest amount that isn't an insult to them, in $5,000 increments. A week later they offered 50k and I started working for them a week after that. The other grant did run out, and I would have been in a bad spot if it hadn't worked out.

I was firm, I knew my market, and I nearly doubled my salary through confidence.

I busted my tail to make sure they got every penny's worth out of me, but when you're confident, when you know you are worth it, when you're bringing value, and have other employment options, you can negotiate for better pay. Starting out, this is a bad strategy because you're not a known commodity and you can't be quite this cavalier. But down the line, when you get some experience and specialized skills, don't think you have to go into poverty in order to work in politics.

Whatever they offer, after you negotiate that amount, still ask for a day to consider it. It's reasonable to ask up to a week to consider it, unless it's the heat of the cycle in the summer before November and it's more reasonable to give a quicker answer. In that time, close out all other offers and potential job offers, figure out if someone else wants to hire you, and put some pressure on them to decide because you have this other offer outstanding. Remember, though, that nothing is final until you have a signed offer letter in your hands. Don't quit your job or even tell your current boss that you're even looking for work until you have that signed offer letter in your hands. An offer letter needs to clarify basics about the job, such as compensation, when you get paid, vacation days, your superior, and your start date. Many campaigns try to avoid offer letters, but if you ask for one, you should get one. And never consider anything finalized, even with an oral agreement with your best friend, until you have that signed offer letter in your hands.

I'm stringent here because I've seen it happen where someone relied on someone's promise (mine) and was let down. A friend was perfect for a job, I gave him the job, my boss approved it and so did all of his superiors, and we thought we were set. Little did we know that a Vice President at the nonprofit decided to veto the decision without notice. He had been working for us for a week when we had to tell him he wasn't ever really hired apparently, because this Vice President decided to go back on our word. You might be saying that surely that wouldn't happen in an age with lawsuits and lawyers and liabilities, but it happens all the time regardless. Most people don't press the issue in court, and quite a few injustices never get prosecuted. Don't rely on your friends' word; they may not have the final control. Nothing is worth acting upon until you have that signed offer letter in your hands.

And there are some places that will just maliciously string you along. On a campaign I was working, the field director was told he had a position with a national presidential campaign waiting in the wings. He mentioned that working for me was always just a temporary thing until this was finalized and opened up for him. I met with the team leader for that campaign and they told me point-blank they would never hire this guy. No one mentioned this to him because the national campaign wanted to keep him volunteering and benefited from stringing him along. After I was no longer with the campaign, I called this guy and told him the truth. I couldn't tell, but it sounded like he was crying as he said goodbye. There's a decent amount of disloyalty by these groups and campaigns towards people beneath them, but they expect their soldiers to bleed for the team. Always protect your own interest. Nothing is set in stone until you get that signed offer letter. Promises by political staffers are almost as worthless as promises by politicians. That idea said another way, "trust, but verify." Don't make your life plans based off of the hopes, dreams, or illusory promises of a campaign.

One other quick related note is to not immediately quit a place, no matter how hard it is in reality; the rule of thumb is to stay a year. Some will say six months, but certainly any less looks unprofessional. A friend once came out to D.C. to work for the summer and spent a week at a place before quitting and going to another non-profit. I didn't recommend him for the position, but it was a very tacky thing to do. You can't approach these working environments like a mercenary always able to side with the highest paying client, you need to have a bit of loyalty to those you're working for, another example of this was a girl who was hired in our department at a political nonprofit. We picked her up from the airport and took her to dinner. While there we had a very nice time, we joked and we were all really looking forward to working with this girl. The next day, she didn't show up for work. We rationalized her absence; we said she must be sick or jetlagged. We didn't think twice.

She missed the next day and the next. We thought it was odd, but didn't get too concerned. By the end of the week it came out that she was quitting, after not even working a single day. A few months later, our boss checked his spam email box and found an email from her, a follow-up to her resignation, where she apparently blamed all of us for her quitting and said that she could never work in that environment.

Clearly, she needed a flight to D.C., took it, and then had another job offer lined up. She better-dealt us for another organization. To a degree, that's defensible because sometimes the perfect place opens up, but the cost of doing that is completely burning your bridges, a risky move in politics. Leaving quickly is very tacky to do, but the email this girl sent with the false accusations was really over the top. We joked for years about the future screaming match we were going to get into with this girl if we ever saw her. You never "need" a job so bad to take whatever one comes along first, and don't accept jobs or operate in bad faith. Be sincere, keep good intentions, check your cynicism at the door, and really try to be a value-added member of a team. You'll get a good job if you apply as a good worker.

ACTION STEPS

1. **Get your 1 page resume together first**
2. **Get some cheap business cards**
3. **Ask your friends and personal network for help, send them your resume**
4. **Bring paper and pen to your interview**
5. **Send handwritten thank you notes**
6. **Prep basic interview questions**
7. **Don't act until you have a signed offer letter**

Chapter 5. Keeping the Job

There are nine good ways to keep your job and actions you can take to protect your continued paycheck in politics. Fundamentally, it all boils down to constantly adding value to an organization. Stay out of trouble, have a good and trusting relationship with your boss and add value, and your chances are enormously better to stay employed.

9 ways to keep your job:
1. Add value to the organization
2. Do what your bosses tell you, and not just the minimum
3. Build up your boss, trust your boss
4. Don't gossip, let your boss know what's going on
5. Be loyal, and let your boss know you're loyal
6. Don't be taken advantage of
7. Try to avoid office politics, but don't become a victim
8. Keep your personal life to yourself
9. Know your weaknesses

Adding value sounds like the typical nonsense that business-ish people bring to politics, a skill-set that is often too regimented and focused to deal with the many creative demands that politics foists upon us. So keep a broad understanding of adding value, and also understand it primarily in terms of adding value that your boss directly understands, appreciates, and perceives.

I hired a fellow at a political job, where my job was starting new publications, and eventually tasked him to do 50 percent video activism, a role that has had major consequences down the line for him, as he was a visionary for using this tactic. The opportunity, if our department and political organization promoted and encouraged this, was huge. My boss understood this completely and was very supportive. His two superiors, though, were dinosaurs technologically and absolutely awful human beings in almost every other respect. Not only did they kill the project and try to fire everyone for even pursuing it, they eventually fired this visionary and made his life hell for at least a year.

Whatever you're doing is pointless if you don't have the overt support of your superiors. It may seem easy to rationalize doing the "right thing" at the time, but if you're later out of a paycheck, the perfect action will seem the enemy of the good action your boss wanted.

The reason I use that anecdote here is that you have to be aware that what you view as value-added is not necessarily what your boss perceives as value-added, or what the ultimate decision-maker perceives as value-added. In another instance, when I was running a campaign and the candidate's wife was nuts about buttons, stickers, and yard signs, I perceived the real needs to be a voter database and good data in general. They were running a grassroots campaign and needed to make every dollar count.

They did not see it the same way, and regardless of my good intent and wise counsel, they controlled my paycheck. These insignificant battles weaken your position and erode your political capital to the point where you can't operate, or worse, you get fired. Keep an eye on what your boss subjectively perceives as value-added, and pursue that primarily. You might be 100 percent right about your desired action, but if it gets you fired it doesn't matter at all. There are very few battles worth fighting that risk your employment.

Most political jobs have one primary decision-maker and one primary metric. Even though they tell you that there are a hundred little things they want you to do and that you're responsible for, and a variety of people to report to, there's usually one thing that takes paramount importance and one person who decides its success. Figure out what that is, and fast, and do that extremely well. At my first political position, I had a plethora of responsibilities including the department's webpage, conferences, letters, and all sorts of minutiae. The primary responsibility, though, was the books and the book publishing. No one ever stated it quite that bluntly, but that's what they really wanted. I could fail at everything else, but as long as that was done right and done well, I would still have a paycheck. Figure that one thing out, and keep your mind focused on performing it well.

On a campaign that might be unstated or assumed. When a campaign hires you to update the website and do their field work, your primary job is often the field work. Primary jobs always relate to the core demands of the organization, and for campaigns and political organizations that always comes back to votes and dollars. What about your job, you should ask yourself, raises more money or influence or turns out more votes? Those are the things to focus on and let the other transient goals get dropped if needed. Keep focused on your real metric.

If you were to over-perform and run out of things to do, you also don't want to be idle and assume that you now have free time to talk to the other staffers or time for personal email. Go to your boss and ask her for guidance, and about how to improve. Anytime you find yourself wasting time at work you should consider how that looks to your boss. It's easy to assume that in a fast-paced environment, especially with young managers, it's easy to not get noticed, but even non-productive interns get noticed. You'll be amazed at how easy it is to tell who works and who doesn't. Keeping and projecting a positive attitude about the work, which is really a way of staying positive about the mission of the group and trusting its management, shines through even on your face.

The old, cliché advice is to always smile when you talk on the phone because people can hear your smile. It sounds corny, but it's true; and it's also true in an office environment. Keep working, avoid idleness and distractions, and focus your work on the one real measure of success for your position.

If you find yourself overwhelmed or burned out during the day, step out to take a break and come back refreshed. One temptation is to always work and "be seen" in a political office, but that's a mistake. You're more than entitled to a small 15 minute break every few hours, and doing so will make the rest of your day that much more productive.

Keep yourself productive and focused on producing. Every moment you waste makes you that much more of a disposable employee. You're being paid for a full day, and so work it and work it hard. Intelligent people often feel as though they can cheat that requirement by "working smarter" and cutting corners or being more efficient. That mentality thrives in business, but politics is another beast altogether.

Most things in politics can't be measured very well, which is why money, polls, and election day votes are overanalyzed. There's always more work to do and always more people to persuade. No matter what kind of political job you're working, never content yourself with doing the minimum or only reaching the goals set for you, always try hard to go above and beyond, to do more than the minimum and do it all at high quality and entirely within the intent of your supervisor.

There's a story about the Nazi leader Martin Bormann, who quickly rose through the ranks to become in the inner-circle at the highest levels of the German government. Outside of the horrible things that these people did, there is an illustrative bureaucratic promotion story to be found here. Unlike Goebbels, who had a skill in writing and communication, or master bureaucrats like Speer or Himmler, there was absolutely nothing remarkable about Bormann. He had no skills, no connections, and was almost entirely unremarkable. The one thing that he did, though, was whenever Hitler made some random comment about a light being out or a small thing he wished were done, Bormann would write it down and make it happen. Obviously, you should be a good person and not emulate Nazis, but there's a strong lesson here that, while we assume merit carries the day, many people get promoted just because they zealously do whatever their superiors want, that's a valuable person to a superior.

I've seen plenty of people follow the Martin Bormann path to political promotion. It's important to distinguish this from brown-nosing or just the typical playing-politics-=by-being-popular. Bormann was never popular and was never well-liked. Most of those around him had very negative things to say about him, but he did what was asked and more. There was an intern at a political non-profit who regularly slept on the job. The kid was a total waste of space. We had him because no other department would take him, and whenever I walked by his cube he was playing some online basketball game, wasting his time.

This former intern has been promoted to upper management and has outlasted everyone else in that department, lacking any qualifications and any relevant experience. I don't think he even worked on a campaign in his entire life. What he did, though, was pursued the Bormann model of advancement and did whatever the Vice President at the time wanted. This opportunist found his chance to get promoted by doing whatever was asked, and being subservient to this superior. It worked like a charm for him; and for Bormann. It's not the right path to success for everyone, and ultimately removes any chance for you to be more than a cog in a machine, so I offer it as more of an illustration of a rule rather than a pattern for you to mimic.

An easy path to advancement is by zealously attending to the needs of your superior. When you ignore the desires of your boss you make it needlessly harder to get promoted.

Remember that bosses don't want advice from subordinates as much as they want their desires implemented. They don't want a discussion and debate about their decisions, they want action that fulfills their thoughts. Serve this role for your bosses, and don't get sidetracked or focus on things other than action. When your boss wants action, deliver in full.

The important thing to consider about that resolute dedication to staying focused on what your boss wants, however, is to also do precisely what your boss or bosses tell you. If you get a weird project or request verbally, ask to have it written out so that it's clear. If you don't understand the project, you won't do it the right way. If you're assuming a certain result, but your boss is expecting something entirely different, you want to be able to rely on what's written down. Many bosses, as well, can forget the exact things they said or remember things wrong weeks later, so having their expectations and deadlines clarified in writing is always best. Keep focused on what they want.

I've been asked to have nerdy students attend a speaking engagement with a former professional wrestler with less than a week's notice during finals, to turn out one hundred students to a training conference with a month's notice, and then to turn out fifty college students to an event during the summer with three weeks notice. I disagreed vehemently with each assignment, I made it known, and then followed my orders precisely. I followed orders and that's what counts most of all.

Everyone in a political office, and everyone on a campaign, will have an opinion about how you should do your job and about your specific projects. It was always entertaining to hear major reform ideas from interns on their second week at a nonprofit, but that's the mentality where intelligent people involved with politics think that the world would run perfectly if only people would listen to them.

You're going to be surrounded by those people, and it's quite easy to get confused about what your boss really wants when many of those around you will be interpreting and explaining "what they really meant" or some other similar comment. It's important when you get this kind of advice that few bosses will ask for complicated tasks without an explanation, and so don't let others make it needlessly complicated. Most things in politics aren't as complicated as they are time-consuming, socially awkward, or expensive. If something sounds complicated, ask for clarification because it probably isn't.

Do what is asked of you, do it well, and complete it on time. If you feel confused, ask for guidance, if you're still confused, ask for it to be put in writing so that it's crystal clear for you and to both of you later. Make sure to do what's asked of you, though. It's a deficiency that often leads to terminations when a new employee cannot do the simple tasks assigned to them, and your coworker's opinion on what your assignment means is often a distraction and rabbit hole that will confuse you more than clarify what's expected.

Never give your boss more work. A management training program I went to in D.C. once described projects and work tasks as monkeys, and explained how monkeys got passed down the chain of command and were never to be passed up. This can seem like a basic point, but let it settle in. You want to make sure not to give your boss more work. Especially with interns, it's a common statement that it's "more time-consuming to explain than it is to just do it themselves."

Don't toss work back up to your boss, and don't expect them to help out. Of course it's always nice when the general fights on the front lines with the privates, but it's never expected. Don't assume or be resentful if your boss has other things going on and can't go out and undertake activities with you and your team.

The advice to be a good employee and not complain is basic but rarely used. The modern tendency abhors work and resists action. Many want to be given elaborate plans, needlessly intricate details, and approval from a dozen bureaucrats before taking a simple action. Be the one who takes the action without complaint, and comes back to your superiors with results rather than problems, keep those monkeys off their back, and report back the completed tasks. That's what your superiors want to hear, that their commands have been executed with no problems and no hang-ups.

> He realized that the way to build a church is not to become entangled in bargains and, to him, rather bewildering questions of legal claim. The way to build a church is not to pay for it, certainly not with somebody else's money. The way to build a church is not to pay for it even with your own money. The way to build a church is to build it. He went about by himself collecting stones. He begged all the people he met to give him stones. In fact he became a new sort of beggar, reversing the parable; a beggar who asks not for bread but stone. - G.K. Chesterton

When you find yourself working on a campaign and are asked to canvass a neighborhood and get 150 new votes and distribute 250 pieces of literature, do it. Don't complain, don't equivocate, don't cheat and don't ask your boss to only do half, and don't gossip to everyone else about why you shouldn't be asked to do such menial things.

Writing that, I realize how basic that must sound in the abstract, here on the page, but the reality on every campaign and in every political organization is that perhaps 40 percent of people will consider themselves potentially "too good" to go out and do the simple things that are asked. Be aware that a college degree, even from a good college, is not meaningful on a campaign. That you studied political science in college does not make you an expert on campaigns; most college classes are entirely inapplicable to elections. If you're a hard worker, if you're used to business, this may all sound shocking, at least until you see it in action and marvel at the audacity of many people who are quite lazy on campaigns and in political organizations.

I have one friend who is the perfect embodiment of this, and the amazing thing is that he works in construction and is far from a lazy person. He's very intelligent, very motivated, college-educated, and is by all accounts a go-getter, but when you ask him to do something on a campaign he finds a way to do it the laziest way or cuts every possible corner and even has the audacity to quote back to you "precisely" what you said so that he's always in the right. Perhaps he is right in some of these instances, but only the most immature of children would consider using a technicality to get out of actually doing the work.

I set a job up for him, one in which he should have made thousands of dollars almost effortlessly given his skills and talents, as a field worker for a political group that paid on performance. This guy, a hard worker, should have thrived. The only requirements were to set up a chapter of this organization, host one small event, and take a few pictures of the event. Instead of doing this the right way and making thousands of dollars, he took the same group of people out to a park, held "protests" for a dozen different groups that were the same people using different group names, took pictures of these different "events," and then was shocked when the organization refused to pay. Sadly, this hurt his case so much that later, when he actually did bust his butt and do legitimate work, they also refused to pay.

The lesson here is twofold: complete not only the specific task asked but follow the obvious intent of your supervisor, and don't stick to a literal interpretation as a way to excuse clearly reckless conduct. Many field workers on a campaign are asked to get petition names, or as in the case of ACORN, voter registrations, and scores always come back fraudulent or erroneously done. Even if you get away with this kind of conduct, it will likely resurface and hurt both you and the organization. Don't try to cut corners, follow the letter and intent of the tasks assigned to you, and do things the right way.

It is always better to underperform honestly than overperform and run the risk of getting caught cheating.

There are good ways to cut corners in politics. If you can get access to an area of high foot traffic and do petitioning there instead of the slow door-to-door method, that's great. If you know, however, that you need to canvass just registered voters and you decide to skip that part and just assume everyone who signs is registered, you're cutting too many corners and not doing what your boss asked.

I'm sure this seems painfully basic, but people are surprised that violations cause terminations. When your superior asks you to do something simple, do it and get that monkey off their back without causing more problems later. Remember that odd advice about monkeys, and don't get rid of one today only to have another reappear tomorrow, keep the monkeys off your boss's back.

90 second primer on **Election Law**

This is **not legal advice**, but it's a good start for asking questions about what can and cannot be done. If you can't find an **election lawyer** on staff, call your local or **state party** and they will find an **election attorney** who can give you advice.

Most basically, almost every "**dirty trick**" is either not worth the potential **legal liability**, or the consequences of the **media** finding out. Hard work wins campaigns, not creative deviousness. Even **stealing yard signs** can be a **federal offense**. **Jamming the phones of a GOTV (Get-Out-The-Vote)** operation is also a **federal offense**. Anything that will be perceived as denying people the right to vote or the ability to vote could incur federal-level problems.

Southern states, in particular, are under a tremendous amount of oversight as to their elections, due to the lingering effects of Jim Crow laws. Any shenanigans in Southern elections are much different than anywhere else in the country because of special federal scrutiny under the Voting Rights Act.

You typically cannot accept any **donations**, cash **or in-kind (free goods or services)**, directly from **corporations** in a **federal election**. Individual contributions over $250 have to be reported to the **Federal Elections Commission**. The FEC can make whatever election rules it wants to, appealing their decisions can take thousands of dollars and years of your life. It's much better to just follow their rules.

If in doubt, always put a **"paid for" box** at the bottom of **everything** on the campaign, your emails, your copies, whatever it takes, it is an easy FEC violation to forget about. It's a crime to send **counterproductive people** from your campaign to the other one as **spies**. It's a technical FEC violation to donate more in-kind time as a volunteer to the campaign than allowable as a financial donation. It's also a crime to give more than the allowable amount and give it to the campaign as an in-kind donation. Most of the regulations about campaigns are **monetary related**. Revenue and expenses in federal campaigns have to be **reported each quarter**, and late filings incur a significant **penalty**.

It's also worth noting that you may be asked to do demeaning things on a campaign, like getting lunch for someone or someone's dry cleaning, often the candidate's. The best advice is to swallow your pride and trust your managers to be professional, even if you're in the right and start complaining about it, it won't help your case. Don't turn into the "gofer" or the one who "goes for" whatever's needed, so that you don't turn into the secretary, but realize that part of paying your dues is doing what's needed at the time. If you can plan it out, it's always wise to do this early on in the campaign so you can "pay your dues" early. No matter how humble you think you are, though, it's always hard to appreciate that your candidate needs to be on the phones fundraising 100 percent of the time, and the time spent ordering chicken sandwiches in line at the fast food joint isn't a good use of their time. Freeing up the time of others on a campaign is a valuable task, and worth doing, just don't make it your main task.

It's also worth doing these small tasks when someone else is pressed for time. The easiest way to get ahead in any office is to finish your work, do well, and then help others succeed and build up a portfolio of IOU's. It's a workplace cliché from the 1990s, but it's wise to be a team player, especially in politics. Those tasks are all part of the success of your candidate and cause, and keeping that focus and working to that end is the mark of a great employee.

You want to build up your boss, and build up your candidate. That's why you free up their time and get stuck running their dry cleaning around. You should trust this person to respect you and appreciate your contributions, even when it seems like they aren't, and this is the person with whom it is most important to keep a good relationship.

Your boss is a protector and a potential promoter. Keeping him satisfied with your work is always the best path to success. Sadly that analysis isn't always a merit-based decision, but the goodwill built with a superior won't mean much if they leave for another position. When your boss turns over, it can be a very dangerous time at any job.

Many political positions are built on a foundation of trust. When new superiors come in, especially if brought in from elsewhere, it's common for them to start with an entirely new team by laying everyone off or bringing their own people with them. Your best protection in this environment, though far from a sure thing, is to keep high numbers and be seen, as I said before, as a major value-added contribution to the team.

When your boss leaves and a new one comes in, make sure that you go out to a one-on-one lunch with the new one within two weeks. Ask her where she sees you, and how you can be the best help to her. New people want to be a success as soon as possible, and want to immediately build a reputation for performance. Said another way, every new boss has something to prove. While it might be tempting to snipe, or be agitated if you were also in competition for that position, realize that the worst thing you can possibly say is that "that's not how we've done things before." If you have a new superior, he has a decent honeymoon period from his supervisors to do almost whatever he wants, and that veritable free hand might include canning you if you are perceived as too uppity.

Work to build the team during a transition. If you don't like the new boss, realize that most political positions last less than a year and many are much shorter. You could get your chance to compete for that position again in a very short period of time. The emphasis is not on your pride or your ego, but on your ability to lead the team and ultimately to affirm and build up your boss.

One poison pill in any team environment is office gossip. It's a team destroyer, and something that's almost always divisive. I'm a sucker for good gossip, but it's almost never a positive presence, and if you enjoy hearing the latest dish you should consider how much you would resent the rumor mill spreading your details around. When you hear gossip, try your hardest to either ignore it or shut it down. There's likely to be a large amount of curiosity and intrigue around the candidate or the organization leadership. This is natural, and it's understandable, but it can be deadly if it festers.

When you hear relevant things, even if they are untrue but relevant because of the suspicion, report the rumor to your boss. Initially, this will seem very wrong, in the sense that you are tattling or "narc'ing" on a coworker. What you are doing, though, is giving vital office information to a manager who needs to know what's going on, and also needs to be able to make many pieces of information floating around work in an understandable whole. You may not appreciate or understand the value of what you're giving them, but it's often very useful and helps people keep jobs rather than getting people fired.

Reporting gossip to your superior can help end suspicions before they begin and can correct problems before they become intractable. There are certain pieces of gossip that, if spread, will permanently change and hurt a working environment regardless of the truth of the rumor. Those kinds of discussions are ones that bring a decent political group to a halt and demolish staff morale.

Be aware of the costs of gossip and help your boss, trust your boss, by reporting the details to them whenever relevant.

You want to be loyal to your boss and make sure that they know you are loyal. Everyone in politics wanted to be president at some point, which means that they psychologically thought that they were the best, the smartest, and the wisest. It is a profession that does not lend itself well to teamwork, trust, and camaraderie. Many people working within politics are in it purely for themselves, just to land a position or to blindly get power. There are many, though, some of the best people you will meet in your entire life, who are involved to help others and truly make a better world. Loyalty to these people, and trust in a working environment, is an entirely right and correct thing.

Communists used to refer to one another as "fellow-travelers" and would have a group of friends wherever they went because of that common bond of principle. Don't be a Communist, but find people who share your principles and desire to help others, and don't be afraid to trust and be loyal to them. Hopefully your bosses can be one of these people, and thus your loyalty to them will be entirely consistent with your philosophical outlook.

An easy point of division and friction is being passed over for a promotion. It can seem as though you earned it, deserved it, had put in the time, or were the most qualified. When you feel this way, it may very well be true, but your only option is to leave and start anew, and it is rarely better to do that than to work harder and smarter where you're at and rise that way. Being passed over can cut deep, but trust that you're being considered for greater things. A friend applied for a job as a driver to a state attorney general, a decidedly entry-level position, but he was so diligent and so hard-working and humble that within a year he had been promoted three times and was earning over double what he started at.

Success in politics isn't complicated, and is often remarkably easy. Its simplicity can be deceptive, it requires patience, endurance, and dedication more than intelligence and creativity.

Being loyal to your boss can quickly pay off; good things come to those who wait and work diligently in the meantime.

One point of loyalty in every political organization is the basic loyalty to the particular political cause. An often unstated rule here is that you are required to vote in every election, in the area relevant to your candidate, campaign, or organization. Ideally, vote absentee so you can take election day off and help out without having to wait in line. No matter how non-political your organization seems, or how unworthy the local candidates, you should always be helping someone local out on election day and making calls or watching polls. This is non-negotiable, and you should take a vacation day off if you must.

In 2006, I sent staffers halfway across the country because there wasn't a serious competitive race for our issue nearby. I wanted everyone to know that elections were that important. Your actions always send a message, as Russell Crowe says in Gladiator, "our actions echo throughout eternity."

Make sure your passion for politics is taking root in each election, especially the local and municipal ones where every vote counts.

Voting is the basic loyalty to your cause, to the organization, and in a basic sense to your boss. It's the public act of demonstrating that you're an effective political operative. There are plenty who fail that very basic idea. I had a fellow who applied for a field position with an organization I was running. He wasn't the right fit for it, but as I was also involved with a statewide referendum in the Midwest I told him I would bring him out there.

As I was a sort of deputy campaign manager for the referendum for a time, it was important to bring people I could trust. I called in some friends and used some favors to bring some extremely talented people along. One fellow I brought, though, became increasingly distant and detached from my leadership and advice over time. Later I discovered that he had been having an affair with another married staffer. Even later I discovered that whenever I would leave he would badmouth my decisions, undercut my actions, and try to lead his own little coup.

The referendum failed, I haven't heard from him since, and I wouldn't recommend the guy for the most basic of entry-level positions. He violated my trust, betrayed my good will, wasted time and resources, and made my other friends very uncomfortable. Even though it was a losing campaign, he could have left with good contacts and a bright future had he not been dishonest and disloyal. The girl who told me of his actions, who always acted with purpose and focus and did what was asked, has my undying gratitude.

Such are the consequences of betraying loyalties and fostering loyalties in politics. Your word and reputation are worth much more than any temporary political rise or momentary opportunity. Especially to your superiors, who almost by definition have more contacts and more opportunities to help you. Stay loyal and stay honest.

When you work it's very tempting to feel taken advantage of, as everyone feels like they're of course worth more than they're being paid. There's some truth to the fear, as many political jobs really do take advantage of you and can stunt your professional growth.

A few quick thoughts on avoiding this unhappy outcome are to overall project value and consider yourself valuable. An easy example here is the trend towards casual wear in office settings. The inconvenience of dressing up for work is often set aside due to the long hours and friendliness of a small team. Ask how that looks, though, and what message that sends to others. Something as small and simple as dressing up and looking sharp projects the idea that you're valuable. People don't send the person dressed the best in the office to grab coffee or lunch, they send the kid in a frumpy shirt and jeans.

Look your best and project value. Owning a $20 iron and using it is an easy way to set yourself apart from other applicants, and other employees. Every employee looks sharp the first two weeks they're on the job, but revert to their real self within four months. After that initial period, stay disciplined and look sharp, you'll stand out as a result.

Being sharp and looking sharp could fill an entirely separate book. Thankfully that book has already been written, "Road to CEO" by Sharon Voros. Look your best and make it easy for others to appreciate your inner talent by looking sharp on the outside.

Keeping that edge also involves making yourself scarce. One tendency and pressure you'll naturally feel is to stay at the office forever into the night. This is a mistake, and one that signals that you have nothing better to do. Leave work on-time, but on a campaign always be on-call.

> "Never mistake activity for achievement." - John Wooden

There are many natural consequences to not leaving work on-time: you'll get lazy, come into work late, miss deadlines, get fat, get frazzled, people won't respect you, you'll be resentful of your superiors, you'll lose control of your social life, your sleep patterns will get upset, and face many other side-effects. A regular, consistent schedule is always the key to success.

If you're always at work and at home only to sleep, it's easy to forget about laundry. There's no way to project value if you're wearing dirty clothes.

By leaving work on-time, you'll be able to avoid these problems by keeping to a regular schedule and having a healthy amount of time to deal with your social life and take care of personal business. If you don't keep a regular schedule, many other things will fall apart.

You want to have your act together. That means managing your life well, having a routine, planning out your finances, and having a plan for your career. It's easy to overlook all of these things when you're young and new to the workforce. It's also easy to accept so much work and get stretched so thin that you're not good at anything. You want to keep everything in check, keep your life in order, and make sure you're not overextending yourself at work.

If your boss comes to you and asks you to do more work, ask to set aside another project or respectfully ask for a larger salary if he is going to put more responsibilities on your plate. You don't want to always accept more work to the point where you're stretched too thin and performing poorly. It's very easy for people in politics to get overextended, and especially for people to burn out.

The main contributing factors to burn out are too much work and not enough free time, working every weekend, and working late into the night every night. When you accept too much work, that's the natural consequence. Financial well-being depends on decent pay, which is often hard to come by, but if you're at an organization for several years, realize that you have to get a regular pay increase just to keep up with inflation. A 5 percent annual pay raise will basically keep pace with your previous salary, but anything less means that you're working for less money each corresponding year. Your target should be a 10 percent pay raise each year, and if you did a great job, don't hesitate to ask for a 15 percent raise.

Money will seem like a replacement for social validation, though, and what's surprising is that most people would forgo a raise in exchange for more appreciation at work from their boss. So if you're feeling unappreciated, ask your boss for a day off and just go to the beach or take a one-day vacation somewhere to clear your mind. Indulge a hobby at home just clear your mind. Take your significant other to a bed and breakfast somewhere, turn off the cell phone, and have a nice time outside of work. Make them miss you instead of your constant anxiety about what's going on at the office or what's happening in politics.

It's tough to get rid of the newshound sense for a weekend, but it can be done. You want to put some distance between you and your work so you can keep perspective.

Otherwise you'll get caught up in the petty office gossip and the latest drama. It's amazing what some organizations can devolve into, a scene straight out of a soap opera.

Keeping distance will make it much easier for you to avoid drama and gossip. You can do well here just by refusing to take a position on the many petty things that become large issues needlessly. It's also wise to just avoid taking a position on entirely subjective questions. If someone has an opinion about the curtains being blue instead of beige, don't weigh in; there's no way to prevail in those circumstances.

Try to keep a circle of friends outside the campaign or organization. You don't want to make your entire life revolve around the job. This also means that, if possible, it's best to live with people other than those you work with. A very good friend was fired from a political organization, and lived with a coworker in the same department. The roommate/colleague began moving his stuff out a week before, and the friend could feel that things were tense at work, made all the worse by him noticing the roommate leaving. It just sets up awkward moments, tense situations; try to keep a separate circle of friends and unconnected roommates.

Also, it goes without saying, that nothing in the world could create more drama than dating coworkers. It's such a natural place to meet people, with the same interests and desires and age, but it is a recipe for disaster every single time. Even when all goes well and wedding bells are on the horizon, it has an effect on the other people in the office environment. As much as possible, try not to date people at work.

It's amazing the kind of trivial things people can focus on in an office setting. Campaigns are all drama all the time, and it slowly escalates as you get closer to election day to the point where the volume is all the way up. But when you notice the office focusing on trivialities, and moving away from a strong work ethic, gently try to reorient them around the task at hand. If you're on a campaign, reorient these people around the idea of getting more votes and winning the election.

That can be tough to do because it's politics after all, and everyone has a zealous opinion about every topic under the sun. It's fun to be in an environment where you can whisper the words "well, I don't really support a ballistic missile shield…" and immediately have a half-dozen people around you violently perk up and start saying you don't want to "protect America." Politics as an interactive sport, as an interpersonal interactive sport, is a lot of fun. Those discussions, though, can kill the work ethic of an office and they can also get under the skin of those who work there. Violent debates sometimes have later consequences.

For as intellectually fun as politics is, it's also inherently divisive, so you want to be careful not to let the division be sown too far. I remember getting into a heated debate at a boss's going away party over the relative benefits and drawbacks of fiction vs. non-fiction works and which was better. People in politics have no compunctions about having that debate, but it can be taken too personally. Those who take it personally will often not come out and say it, either, so it can hurt you later and you won't even know it.

One good way to ease the tension, especially when surrounded by political animals, is to host social nights with politically-themed movies. I mentioned a few of my favorites before, but there are some classics that many haven't seen. Most are relatively bipartisan gems, so you can even invite people of different political persuasions and have a nice time. Classics like *Dave*, *Mr. Smith goes to Washington*, *The Distinguished Gentleman* and *Wag the Dog*, or a more partisan *Primary Colors* and *Bulworth*, are all worth a good movie night and discussion.

These movie nights can help you be social with coworkers, while still keeping some distance between you and work. You want to keep your personal life to yourself.

If you have a bad breakup, keep it to yourself and away from work. Call in sick and just take a personal day if you need to; it's not worth getting everyone else involved with your personal life. I've made some pretty amazing mistakes here. It's not hard for people to see that you're an emotional trainwreck, so spare them the awkwardness of witnessing it and get your mind right.

I had a job where I gave skills workshops to college students, and after breaking up with my college girlfriend, a week later I was on the road again giving these workshops. Well, I didn't even notice it at the time, but a student I befriended casually mentioned years later the multiple times I referenced the relationship and talked about this girl during the workshop. Tacky, tacky, tacky! I should have taken a day or two off and gotten my head straight. Even though I wanted to get focused on work, I was not doing good work because I wasn't thinking straight.

Being productive and a positive influence at work is more important to the employer than being an iron man.

A few years and a different girl later, I was at a major annual event sitting at a bar at the end of a long day with some major donors. My girlfriend at the time, with whom I was in a pretty serious relationship, was fighting with me over something trivial. She came into the bar and sat at a distant table facing me, with the major donors in my midst. I offered some tepid response, but over several hours that night it became an increasing source of tension and was obvious that we were having relationship issues. There's so much wrong with that situation I don't know where to begin. I should have politely excused myself. You're definitely not putting your best foot forward, and doing harm to your work, to the relationship with the donors and not fixing the personal relationship either.

Don't let your personal life and your work life mix, try to keep them as separate as you can. Many people meet future spouses on campaigns, so I don't mean to say ignore the people around you, but inter-office romance comes at a high cost, seen and unseen. Proceed with a great deal of caution before entering one.

If it happens, be conscientious about keeping the drama and the displays of affection out of the workplace, treat one another as professionals, and try to keep all your personal business to yourselves.

You keep the personal and professional separate because relationships are always messy, and it's easiest to contain the damage this way. It's a way of knowing your own weaknesses and planning for when things don't go exactly right. Working in politics and being active on a campaign works the best when you know who you are and can plan for the worst.

If you're a smoker, don't try to quit while on a campaign. Indulge your vices and quit the day after the election. If you have a bad habit, don't obsess over it and focus on it. Keep focused on the work and the impending election instead.

If your problems, bad habits, and vices are getting too much notice, do things to break people of that idea. If you always show up late to work, come in early from now on. If you're always looking sloppy and disheveled, then come into work with a nice outfit for a week or two. You do those things to break them of their stereotype so that their nitpicking doesn't become a distraction or a problem for you later; you do it so that you can focus on what really matters: election day.

Since you've perhaps had the bad habit for a long time, it's tough to be wholly introspective on these things. And getting honest feedback can be difficult since everyone is so used to spin, diplomacy, and glad-handing that they'll just affirm your vices. Don't be surprised if all you hear is positive comments, but you know that people are talking behind your back about your bad habits. If you hear about it, it's a problem; and if you're hearing about it, your boss is likely hearing about it, which means you need to fix it.

Know your weaknesses, work on correcting them, and fix them. All of your problems have solutions, and being in a solid culture of self-improvement will ease this process.

When you're in a new job, or in many cases in a new place altogether, you're very vulnerable. Other people want your job and everyone is a competitor. Make friends and get to know people outside work, get to know people who can give you good feedback, who can tell you if you're crazy. Especially on a campaign, you need to get to know people just for the feedback, so that you're not always feeling stressed and under the gun. Everyone has eccentricities and problems, so you want honest feedback on the weird things other people do, and the weird things you're doing that are obnoxious to others. Friends help you do that when they're not coworkers.

ACTION STEPS:

    1. Make a project list you can work on at all times.

Chapter 6. Doing Well at the Job

17 ways to do that:

1. Keep working
2. Work even when others don't
3. Don't listen to what others say, do what your supervisors say
4. Be wary of power struggles
5. Stick to your own long-range plan, don't plan to stay somewhere forever
6. Add value to the organization and to yourself
7. Protect yourself
8. Watch out for vendors
9. Avoid workplace relationships
10. Watch out for the family of your boss
11. Get better at fundraising
12. Get better at technology issues
13. Get better at event planning
14. Get better at data and statistics
15. Get better at writing
16. Get better at being on the phone
17. Get better at public speaking

A large part of this book is focused on this topic, doing well, which might seem odd for a book ostensibly about getting the job and not about excelling at one. But the problem one sees all too often is not the inability to get a good job, but in keeping one. If you can project a good face and focus on your value to the candidate or group, you can get a job. But politics has a significant turnover rate, and keeping the job can prove to be the most challenging aspect.

Because jobs end, organizations fold, and people often get canned, you need to constantly be doing well to get the recommendations for the next job.

The suggestions here will seem intuitive, but they are often discarded in the heat of the moment. Don't let the stress of politics make you lose sight of these basic ideas that will save your paycheck when you need it the most.

First of all, keep working. It's easy to get sucked into the drama and routine of always putting out fires. You need to identify your core metrics, or measurable things that you're being asked to do on a regular basis, and do those things first and foremost. This can be tough to do when you rationalize solving major problems on a day-to-day basis. And the fires never stop coming, so write out your goals. Even if your boss hasn't stated them, write them out for yourself anyway.

And if you find yourself still fighting to keep focused on those core metrics, start keeping a detailed time sheet during your day. This will seem monotonous and excessive for sure, but doing so and reviewing it at the end of the day will show you where your time is going, and where it's being wasted or diverted. Compare your major goals and real metrics with the amount of time you're allocating to those projects daily, and the problems will jump off the page at you. As this is tedious and time-consuming in itself, you don't have to do this for weeks on end to get the desired results, but doing it for a few days will yield the results you need to make an honest self-assessment.

As a fan of written-out plans, I'd also suggest writing one out to yourself that theorizes paths for you to get ahead. On a campaign, what's a goal that no one has reached before, or would be truly amazed to see? Perhaps it's a record number of absentee ballots, or recruiting and leading a phone bank for voter identification or basic voter contact over a period of time. Figure out what your goal is, and then sketch out ways to get there, and follow the plan. As the cliché goes, a plan always beats no plan, and you want a plan to get ahead.

Within organizations, this can be a bit more difficult, but only because many people within these groups stay entrenched in safe roles for years on end. New things are often met with hostility despite your best intentions. But if you want to be a nonprofit president and you're 25 without a degree and working in the mailroom, what separates you from that position may seem insurmountable, but it is not impossible. Using that extreme example, just looking at the career history of the organization's president or candidate for your campaign is likely illustrative of what you need to do to reach the same level of success.

Perhaps they have a graduate degree in a specific field, perhaps they, themselves, once ran for a lower office. It may seem odd, but it's surprisingly rare to find people active in politics who have run for office themselves, most prefer to be an operator and work behind the scenes. You can easily stand out by running for something, and even if you lose, you'll still get a lot more respect than you otherwise would have had.

The board, for example, may require a degree or a certain number of years of experience at the organization for a senior position. Perhaps they desire to promote from within and also prefer people who have run a winning state senate race. Whatever their requirements are, they're eminently reachable if you put your mind to it, write out your plan, and figure out how to run your plan.

No job is impossible to get. You might want to create false requirements for the position, exaggerating what you really need to do in order to be promoted to that level, or say that you have to outdo the person currently in the position, but more often than not just fulfilling the same requirements and having the same general resume will make for a perfect replacement once the current person vacates your ideal spot.

But most people never make this analysis and prefer, instead, to think purely in the short term and harbor resentment that they're so much smarter than their boss and have so much more experience and yet never get promoted. These are people without a plan, and the discipline to write it out and run with it. And they stay stuck in that situation because they never objectively list out what they need to get ahead. Most careers in politics are full of lackluster accomplishments and relatively little that would truly impress you. Those that do make outlandish claims are usually pathological liars. Trust me, I've met a few. So, building a plan to get good experiences and decent successes oriented around what your ideal job is will yield the right promotion if you stick with it.

And if it doesn't, some other upstart campaign or non-profit will take notice.

The second piece of advice here is to work even when others don't. This, as well, may seem obvious. But it's so tempting in a field dependent on being social and sociable to engage the issues, discuss the problems, indulge political passions and debates, and revisit the nuances of the news. The impact of this will be to kill productivity even when people don't realize it. The day will whittle away and no one will be doing their job, nothing will get done, but everyone will think that work was done because politics was discussed in the office all day long.

I've done this a shameful amount. When considering how many elections I've seen affected by a few hundred votes, it puts it well into perspective. Your idle banter might mean the difference between winning the election and losing, between your cause prevailing and being set back several years.

Living a workplace full of ideas and debate is fun, but is unproductive and the mark of a loser. Said another way, "losers don't legislate."

Constant office debate will be terminal to your career and the employment of others. My best advice is to take out a post-it note and write out the project you're working on and place it above your workspace and to stay focused on that specific project until it's done. Don't flirt with the new hottie, don't check the web for all the latest news, don't obsessively check the Drudge Report for up-to-date headlines, instead, do the work you are supposed to be doing.

I know others who are diligent about not checking email except at specific times such as 10am, 2pm and 6pm while they're focused on a major project. We live in a very short-attention-span kind of environment, and your work habits are no doubt a partial reflection of that culture, so do what you can to stay focused, and focused on that which matters: the major projects you need to get done right away. Minimize your distractions.

Remember that a thousand people want your job at any given moment, and other politically ambitious people would love to knock you off and take your job or give it to one of their friends. I was running a senate race and a former aide to the lieutenant governor, a director of the college political network across the state, was daily asking my candidate to fire me because of an old grievance between him and the brother of my then-girlfriend that I had absolutely nothing to do with. It probably had nothing to do with me, I suspect he just had a friend whom he wanted in that position, and I didn't rank high on his list of favors.

Welcome to politics, where those within your own party often seem like the real enemy. But remembering that this fellow was constantly after me was also a good motivator. During the 1960 campaign, Kennedy was reported to always have a sign nearby that said Nixon is probably sleeping an hour less, resting a little bit less, and working just that much harder for every bit of comfort you give yourself. You don't need that kind of stress and anxiety, but you'd benefit more from a little extra of it than too little of it.

Keep yourself motivated and your work ethic strong.

Your individual work ethic is paramount, and this might seem like a challenge, but you also want to be careful not to overdo it, or overperform. Teamwork and being part of a team also means advancing at the same rate as everyone else.

This is not what you learned in economics.

You want to excel, you want to stand out, but you don't want to be so good that you become hated by everyone else. If you overperform at making widgets, use your extra widgets to give to the lower performers, establish your front place status, and help others succeed. This, as well, is not advice that applies in business as much as it does in politics, because violations of this advice will see you as the most productive person in the office who still ends up getting fired because the rest of the team poisons the well for you to succeed.

No one likes working in a team where they're always going to be second place. You can stand out without always beating everyone else.

I was working at a place and broke the record for widgets by over 200 percent, and a friendly mentor-type pointed out the error I'm relaying to you, causing me to downgrade my accomplishment into merely breaking the record by a bit. It was sage advice, and helped me look great to upper management, but also didn't alienate me completely from the team I was working with.

Also, if you do too well, many people will naturally become suspicious of your numbers. If you break the record by double, even by working three times longer and harder, some will still see it as suspicious and that won't help you in the long run either. Break the record by a little bit and you won't have to worry about that kind of frustrating scrutiny. I once worked with a fellow who had claimed he single-handedly collected 6,000 absentee ballots for a candidate in a 10-week period, an amazing feat.

Later, after his multiple arrests and unbelievable workplace drama, all of those claims were shown to be lies. He was breaking the records by too much, he was overperforming and not keeping expectations in line. Overperform just a little bit and you can avoid the scrutiny.

It's always wise to remember that most political jobs involve "paying your dues" as some sort of abstract and unapplied rule, but what that really means in practice is surviving and enduring despite the drama, high demands, and potential landmines that are daily in your way. And this is an extremely delicate balance, as I said you want to do well, but not too well. You want to be the best on your team, but you don't want to shame the others. Getting ahead also means, in terms of "paying your dues," that you invest some more hours and work to justify that promotion. Just doing your job, though, isn't sufficient for that promotion. You need to excel, but keep it within the bounds of reality otherwise you'll breed contempt for the staffer whose baby kept them up at night, who lives above a bar and never gets a good-night's sleep, or who just had a fight with her boyfriend and isn't focused.   Remember that you're part of a team, and help that team advance while you're at the top of the pack.

All that junk in middle school about being a "team player" does have some small, practical application.

One of the distractions that often pulls people away, other than their personal problems, is the peculiar political penchant for avid scheming in all things. You'll see this all the time, people scheming to start their own nonprofits, or people scheming to start their own mail houses, an event, an activism project, a long-shot campaign, or people scheming on how to develop new fundraising lists that they can sell to everyone and make millions. Part of the genuine thrill and fun of politics are the crazy schemes that develop in what seems like every other conversation.

A million schemes are active at any point between a hundred thousand people in politics, ten to a man. Each one is more outlandish than the next. But these schemes will all seem logical, reasonable, and realistic when you hear the coworker in the cubicle next to yours lay it out over late-night coffee. But these schemes are all distractions from your central job.

Stay focused on your job and work even when others don't.

The schemes will seem like your next meal ticket, they'll seem like the next world-changing affair. And true enough, I've had $700,000-a-year nonprofits evolve from schemes hatched on napkins over chicken wing dinners in Vienna, Virginia and long-running schemes on video activism with another friend eventually lead to major news coverage and major political action, but for every one successful scheme there are 100 that died and were a total waste of time.

When you are on a campaign, and when you are new to politics, these schemes are almost always a total waste of your time. Indulge them as your ego demands, but realize that your best path to success both long-term and short-term is through excelling at your job and keeping that steady paycheck.

Schemes cannot pay the rent, and most of the real schemes that work out are the ones that become funded through major donors, not through some crazy idea of how to raise money from turning lead into gold, or getting a thousand clients to sign up for some brand-new service off of a crazy excel list we threw together, or reselling campaign merchandise at 90 cents on the dollar to campaigns by getting it cheap from some deadbeat cousin of yours.

Stick around, you'll have plenty of crazy ideas come your way, and remember my advice to work even when others don't.

The third piece of advice here is to do what your supervisor says and not what others tell you. The challenge here is getting an accurate read on your boss and not having your boss's intentions contextualized solely by the prejudices of everyone else. Molly Ivins used to say to "dance with the one that brung ya, and in your case remember to dance with the one that hired ya."

Ask yourself who your boss is and what your boss wants. There aren't that many types of bosses, and it's relatively easy to say what kind of bosses you have, and from that, figuring out how to give them what they want.

Let's first identify a variety of boss "types" as:

1. the reluctant politico
2. the a-type businessman
3. the policy wonk
4. the non-political trustee
5. the young go-getter

Let's also consider a variety of common novice errors when it comes to bosses, especially on matters as subjective as politics. First off, don't bitch about your boss in front of his subordinates, and don't correct him or offer false praise or sarcasm. Even when you have a good relationship or have been friends for a long time, keep that stuff private. Inside jokes, gibes, taunting and teasing, so tempting to do in front of others, should really be left for one-on-one situations instead. You don't know the relationship he has with other people, and you're giving license to others to treat him that way when you act unprofessional. Keep a positive, active, and affirming face when it comes to your boss in front of other people, even though that can be quite difficult at times.

Also assume that anything you say to your boss gets repeated to her boss, and that everything you say to your boss's supervisor travels down to your boss as well. Meaning that there are few secrets, and you should presume there are zero, between the two people in the chain of command above you. Never ever play the game of trying to outmaneuver your boss by going above her and complaining for trivial matters, as I guarantee it will backfire. And in the off-chance it does succeed, you only guarantee that it will later happen to you, and you'll have made a mortal enemy in your now unemployed boss.

I've had several people do this to me, and it never really worked out for them, but I'm still, years later, always a half-step away from declaring global jihad against them. I would readily forgive a cheating girlfriend sooner than I would a cheating employee who ruins and interferes with my relationship with my supervisor. Avoid the temptation to meddle here, and save yourself the trouble.

Don't add your boss as a friend on Facebook, and certainly don't add your boss's supervisor as a friend on Facebook. Old people love to "friend" people now that they've figured out this newfangled website, but it's also a recipe for disaster. I knew a girl who just put all her bosses on "limited" view, but that just seems both dishonest and potentially problematic. Save yourself the trouble and don't include them at all.

Fourth, be wary of power struggles. With political jobs come the natural office politics and the jockeying for promotion and position that people undertake. When these things happen, just stay uncommitted and uninvolved. Focus on your job, minimize the scheming, and don't attach onto any faction, just stay the company man who does the job diligently. One major reason to avoid committing yourself is that it's so easy to guess wrong and to make the wrong assumptions.

Once I had an awful relationship with my supervisor, a man whom I had a previous friendship with and yet, despite that prior history, we could not agree on a single thing that advanced my work. Moving forward, I felt that it eventually became so contentious that I had to report my boss's mistakes to his supervisor, and help those trying to remove him. I made one comment to his boss, and never heard anything more. Three years later, long after we were both employed elsewhere, over beers he explained to me that he was largely exasperated with defending me to his boss, and that it was his boss who was the one who was really making my life miserable. It all made sense, and what he was saying fit all the pieces of evidence.

I had guessed wrong, and from my vantage point it seemed so clear that my boss was the problem. I was about to quit that job in a huff I was so upset, yet my boss quit two weeks later instead. But from your position as an entry-level employee, as someone who isn't privy to the higher-level conversations and struggles, be careful before involving yourself in these power plays because it's so easy to guess wrong and have it result with you unemployed on the curb.

Power struggles also sap your energy, morale, and time. It will make you a bad employee overnight. As I mentioned before about the office devolving into discussion groups about current events, so it can become seriously unproductive during power struggles. It just becomes a suck of energy and time, so staying focused is the real key to surviving these situations the best. There's no way to "win" or plan these things out, or control the many unpredictable potential problems, so try as much as possible, to let your work speak for itself and not get dragged down by these major flare ups of office politics, and avoid the haters.

Fifth, stick to your own long-range plan, and don't plan to stay somewhere forever. It can become tempting to work at a place and let that familiarity and security develop into a modification of your plan that involves working at that place for a long period and become a career person at the particular organization, and in that way you modify your plans get wrapped around the institution rather than you wrapping the institution around your plans. You want to be the unmovable force and your plans the realization of your real dreams rather than subordinating your dreams to the institution.

Institutions, and especially campaigns and candidates, are fickle things. They change their minds, they run out of money, they become different people when they get elected. If your plans revolve around your candidate getting elected and becoming a career servant to the candidate, which could be a good outcome and reach your goals, it's too delicate in practice because so many things can go wrong with that plan. You want to use your work experiences and your jobs to help you reach your goals and enable your own fulfillment. For me, I wanted to help build organizations, as I've always enjoyed that process. Similar to the same personal satisfaction felt by a teacher, I love watching something grow up out of nothing. The places I've worked reflect that, and the places I was at for an extended period of time, without that element, were unfulfilling. But much of what I did that I enjoyed didn't match a specific plan, or connect well together, I just floated between positions that worked at the time and didn't consider how that lead to a larger goal.

And that requires a lot of serious introspection and consideration about who you are. I wanted to be a million things, and my interests were in a thousand different places, so it became difficult to become great at one thing, and to be the best in my field at one thing because I was unfocused. Your long-range plan, in as much as you have one or can have one, ought to provide the discipline to reject certain types of jobs, and help you realize what works within your plan and what doesn't. When you work in politics for more than a few years, you want your experiences to coalesce around your primary goals; you want them all to come together.

After all, most people stay about 2 years at any given position, and 50 percent get fired from their first job. It's very possible that your position in politics will not be lasting, so make it work for you rather than imagining that your position is permanent. That transition, the idea of leaving a secure place, is a difficult one to grasp at the time and easy to take for granted when you're in the middle of the job search. When you're seeking employment, you're busy weighing your options and objectively looking at your possibilities. But when you're in a place, you idealize it, and you become too comfortable with it.

The comfort leads to apathy, mediocrity, and complacency. You want to be in a constant mode of critical self-evaluation and self-improvement. There's a fabulous book I mentioned before that you ought to read that puts you in performance mode, *Road to CEO* by Sharon Voros, an executive headhunter who shows what companies look for in sharp professional people. This is the kind of person you want to be in politics.

And that culture of self-improvement can be brutal. Are you fat? Plan out how you can shed those pounds and wear clothing that is most flattering to you. Are you sloppy? Find ways to become more organized. Are you a bad writer? Practice and get better; find a blog to contribute to where you can find an editor who will work with you to improve your writing. Almost any problem has a solution. Even things that seem insurmountable sometimes have easy and obvious solutions. Always forgetting to put on deodorant in the morning? Leave an extra stick in your car and in a drawer at work for the times you forget. For whatever odd problem you have, there is often an easy solution.

You want to improve yourself; you want to become a political professional, someone who is respected, and an automatic presence and authority when entering a room. Become your best person; you have it within you.

As you are constantly adding value to yourself, you are also constantly adding value to your employer. And they'll notice this change, this major difference from those who go to work just to collect the paycheck, or who treat their social and personal life as so separate and distinct from their work life as though it has no effect on the other.

How you improve yourself is also how you are improving the company, the campaign, or the operation you're with.

Bringing that value to the organization is something you should do all the time. The sixth main point is to always be adding value to the organization and to yourself. And that culture of self-improvement seems tough at first, but once you get used to it, becomes second nature. An easy, and seemingly tough one, is to turn off the television. It's the greatest time-waster in society, and has little to no redeeming value. You might think that it provides some kind of social bond or unity with coworkers, but it doesn't. The best and most professional people I know either don't watch or completely lack a television altogether. I gave mine up five years ago and haven't missed it since, it's been a wonderfully liberating opportunity to focus on the things I really care about, and have the disposable time to myself so that more of my personal life didn't spill over into work.

Another way to bring value is to attend functions and find out what's going on with other groups, other campaigns, as well as the general man on the street opinions. Make sure to go to all the political functions you can; if you have a free night, fill it with an event. Even the boring ones, those you've been to before, can often yield a small nugget worth considering. And if you're afraid that the event will be a bust or a total waste, bring a blackberry to text discretely or bring something to write with and outline a press release, write an article, or schedule your next day. It's generally much better to write than read something in an obvious fashion because you could appear to be taking notes on the event or speech instead of doing other work. If it's likely to be a boring event, bring something to write with and on, and sit in the back and do this so it's not a total waste.

Big fundraising dinners can be the worst. I was at one where a variety of speakers, many political science professors from local colleges, were giving these ridiculously lofty and airy speeches to a room of about thirty people. I actually took a date to this event, who made the astute observation that what had obviously happened was that they invited everyone locally who could potentially speak, and couldn't say no when they all accepted. It was quite a grueling series of blasé political speeches, but having something to write with allowed me to draft press releases as I sat in the back.

In addition to political functions and fundraisers, you should also try to attend as much political training as you can handle. Some call this "political technology," the kind of skills that are essential to success in politics such as media, fundraising, public speaking, data management, recruitment, among many others. For both political sides, there are plenty of national, state, and even local training outfits and opportunities. Your best bet to get word of them is to call your state party, who will likely know of most going on in your area, as well as statewide political groups existing in most states.

These training workshops won't make you a master at the skill overnight, but repeated exposure to them, and repeated exposure on the same topics, will make you much more comfortable with those skills later, and, added to your resume and known around your office, will greatly enhance your value both personally and to the organization. You're probably saying to yourself that by this point you are a great public speaker, and you know how to recruit, and you've done fundraising before.

This is the exact mindset that you need to get out of, and even training workshops which you have been through before are ones you should attend again because you'll confront the information with prior knowledge. You'll see the application much more the second time around, rather than the base information. Reviewing the same material and going through the same training will allow you to master it, internalize it, and appreciate where to apply it within your position.

I worked for a training outfit that had 34 different courses, and I took each one I could as often as I could, and learned something new each time. I left with reams of notes that, even now, years later, I'm still going through and implementing. You can't underestimate the importance of these training sessions, and the opportunity they present to you to add value to yourself, and subsequently to your political organization.

The seventh way to do well at keeping your job is to take active steps to protect it, and to protect your situation. Especially when you perceive workplace tension aimed in your direction, consider a few steps to survive a political organization's tendency to let people go easily. This means always finishing your work, and always taking requests from your supervisor seriously. I've had several employees who, perhaps because of my age at the time, considered my requests optional. I would ask for very basic and clear things, and their option was always to verbally accept and then ignore it, even catching one who later bragged to others that I never followed up with those things I gave her.

And I didn't follow up not because of some inherent organizational defect, but because I trusted her to the point where I felt like I didn't need to follow-up. In a moment, in an instant, she ruined that trust and ruined our working relationship by not finishing her work and keeping diligent track of it.

Always keep the boss's tasks written down and easily accessible. After all, the boss might be inadvertently overloading you with work and you need to communicate that. And always keep the deadlines, either express or implied, to those tasks in front of you as well. Meet your deadlines and don't require nagging and the kind of micromanagement that becomes exhausting on you and your supervisor. I had an intern whom I overworked, and one helpful method for her to stay on top of things was to keep a list of all that was being assigned, and then to separately make a list of the things she was going to work on for the day and to rank them in order of priority. At first, this seemed pedantic to her, but in time, diligently doing this day after day, it gave her the discipline and focus not to stress about the tasks in front of her. Instead of seeing that large pool of tasks, she could focus on what was realistically in front of her.

After that, she was less stressed and was completing tasks in a strong, consistent, and reliable fashion. It worked great. Always take requests and assignments from your supervisor seriously.

I had a superior at a job who, in the first week, assigned two tasks to everyone. One of the tasks was trivial, something like doing his dry cleaning or grabbing him a coffee. And the second task was something large and grandiose, something that required true vision. From these two tasks, he told me several years later, he quickly determined from the trivial request if people would simply do what he asked, a most important trait among employees. The grandiose task would tell him if these people trusted his judgment in such a fashion as to attack big dreams with the patience, dedication, and focus needed to realize them, even if they never came to life.

Keep a list of the things assigned to you by your boss, treat them with respect, and seriousness; if you overlook them or treat them with disrespect, that decision can have serious consequences in the workplace. It shows that you work as part of their team, and that you follow directions. And that comes with certain subtleties as well, such as not over-performing in your role so as to shame the rest of the workplace and using any over-performance to help those who are struggling. You protect yourself in the challenge of keeping your job by treating your boss with respect and working as part of your team as a hard-working, extremely productive individual who leads the pack but still cares about the success of everyone in an operation.

Working hard, and having other useful skills, helps you build those relationships essential to success in an office setting. Obviously, you can't please everyone, and some will always dislike or resent you for whatever reason, but you can help as many people as possible with their workplace problems and engender a good degree of positive feelings and potential favors to cash in later. Work with your coworkers and succeed together, and help them with the things they need.

This helps keep the relationships and personal drama to a relative minimum. It keeps people focused on a positive attitude towards you, and prevents gossip from becoming too nasty towards you if you have people who appreciate the things you have done for them. It's a way to contain natural resentment and office gossip and drama; it's a productive, active way to forestall drama. Few things are as pointless and frustrating in an office setting as the kind of office drama deriving from personal relationships gone awry.

The avoidance of that needless drama is also dependent on your own ability to contain the problems within your personal and social life, to keep the natural hiccups from becoming your boss's problems. When those things happen, it can often feel normal and natural to share them with those at work, those you spend so much of your time around, but it's a mistake almost every single time. It introduces an element to your work life that you want to zealously keep separate; you don't want your boss to know your love life and give relationship advice. It puts her in an uncomfortable position, and demonstrates that you perhaps don't have full control over your emotions and physical passions.

Keep all personal issues and problems, with those at the workplace and those in your private life, completely out of and separate from the workplace. Another easy and seemingly obvious tactic is to buy a cheap stack of thank you notes from CVS or Walgreens, and write thank you notes to coworkers when they help you with something or help run an event that you were involved with. It's amazing how rarely this is done, and how easy it is to do. I buy these packs several at a time, and, admittedly, I rarely hear back from people when I send these notes, probably because it's so rare that they're sent out, but in the times that I have gotten responses the recipient has been grateful. Giving people acknowledgment and thanks at work is often what most people desire most: they want to feel appreciated and valued.

These tactics and efforts will only go so far, however, and certainly times will arise that even the political capital you've amassed among the staff and with your boss may not save you. And the wise political operative will have a patron, a person of authority who can protect you and your position. This person is ideally a major donor or a board member. It's a common misperception that campaigns don't operate by committee or that there isn't some central steering board. Many campaigns have these, either overtly or somewhat unstated, where there are those involved with the campaign who have influence, even over the candidate. Politicians are, after all, interested primarily in their reelection, and those who have power over those reelections are well respected by the candidate.

Having one of these patrons as a close friend, and as someone who can take an interest in your career and advancement, is very valuable. Tangibly, these people are, as I said, people with power over the reelection of the candidate or with influence over the organization. And as I've said elsewhere, almost all of politics revolves around votes and money, the primary types of people who can then naturally have that influence are: major donors, media bigwigs, corporate heads, union leaders, interest group leaders, religious leaders, other politicians, celebrities, and the like. People who have a natural constituency, and can bring significant items of interest to the politician's table, namely votes and money.

A strong person who fits this description who is solidly in your corner can make all the difference in the world when you get into a tight spot. It's tougher, but not impossible, to rely on them when you get into a serious problem of your own making, but especially during tough moments they can be the difference between having a paycheck in the future and looking for work again. They can also prevent you, even if they can't save your job, from being badmouthed or defamed after you leave as the campaign or political organization will want to keep good relations with this patron.

After being on the losing end of a power struggle, I had a patron like this create a position and small interest group for me as a job for a project he was interested in. It was amazingly considerate, kind, and generous of him, and I was certainly not entitled to that kind of accommodation, but it was a very kind gesture and one I won't forget. I lost a position at a separate organization when the patron I had fell out of favor, losing my position almost a month afterwards. Clearly, that protection kept me in the position much longer than I would have been without that help.

That protection extends to office politics and the insignificant drama, but times will obviously arise when you have made a mistake, or inadvertently made a mistake, that lacks a clear or sufficient explanation, or perhaps your entirely valid explanation is too fantastic to be believed. Things happen, and after it happens it's often impossible to undo. So, the best protection after the bomb has gone off is to immediately go to your supervisor and talk it over. As difficult as it might be, confess your mistakes to your supervisor. Just like Watergate, the crime comes with the cover-up not as much with the crime itself. Your boss is a problem-solver, and all of my supervisors have been considerably more tolerant of mistakes than I thought they would be; they've had the same jobs you've had and mistakes are often just part of the job.

The worst situation is when others tattle on you, and it looks like you were keeping something from your supervisor. The natural tendency, derived from pride, ego and natural immaturity, is to not report a problem until you've completed the solution. In politics, this is the wrong way to look at things; you want to involve your supervisor in the consideration of the right potential solutions to the problem at hand. Even if you negligently created the situation, there are reasonable solutions that you might be overlooking.

After all, this problem has likely come up before. No problem you run into can be truly unique, and crazy things happen in politics all the time. Trust your boss to have the big picture, and experience, to manage a small crisis and help weigh the various options available to correct the problem. It can also seem natural to involve coworkers with the solution, but this, too, is a mistake. You want to give your supervisors the position, authority, and control to involve whomever they decide to involve, and not take that decision away from them.

Working in book publishing once, I made a rash decision that resulted in a $4,000 mistake. I went to my supervisor, as a new employee almost positive that I was going to be sent packing, and reported this to her. After several long sighs, she weighed the options, discussed how to prevent this in the future, and told me not to do it again. I was amazed, but later in a management role I realized how valuable employees are, and how greatly managers want to work with the team to succeed. They aren't going to fire people for trivialities, and while repeated mistakes add up, and there are plenty of nonsensical firings in politics, you're much more likely to be fired for covering up a mistake and it being found later, or being found through office gossip, than if you handled it the right way by taking it to your supervisor.

Being forthright about mistakes is key to resolving those disputes, but it's also wise to always be scrupulously honest about numbers that you use in politics. Professionals can always see through the bull handed to them by professionals. Claiming that you single-handedly collected 8,000 absentee ballots for an election is a statistic I've heard and knew was baloney. Hearing people say that they run three nonprofits simultaneously, another gem I've heard, was also obvious crap. I was at a small meeting at the White House once, with six other nonprofits involved in political work, each with larger budgets than the one I was running. I was with a confident director who worked for me, and I instructed her on the same lesson here. And as the groups went around the room reporting their statistics, they all discussed their influence in the scale of the millions they were in touch with. They were each like peacocks puffing out their feathers and each feather had millions of contacts. It could easily have been intimidating.

We took half the time during that meeting discussing our group because we were honest and of interest to the rest. It was a small coup founded on our decision to let our work speak for itself.

This wise director, though, accurately reported our statistics, in the few hundred campus groups we had, the reliable emails we communicated with, and the student leaders we worked with. In comparison to the other groups and their claimed stats, we were small specks. But the difference was that our numbers were real, we didn't use numbers wastefully, we had a real ground game, and we did serious grassroots organizing. The entire room was asking about our numbers, and not with a dismissive or patronizing tone, but with the genuine interest of those who wanted to know more upon hearing real numbers. This is the kind of respect you want to project, and with a reputation for accuracy and honesty, it will make you rise quickly.

Anyone can lie about numbers that can't be checked. But honesty and realistic performance, demonstrating hard work and sustained work, is of interest to everyone. It's a novice mistake to lie about your resume, float your statistics, and bloat your performance. Once you get the reputation as someone who talks like this, as well, you can never undo it, and will always provoke skepticism in your numbers. With donors, coworkers, and especially your boss, always be honest and give them the accurate read on things.

Even when you commit a negligent mistake, keep that honesty. When you notice it in others, keep that honesty. Another time, I was an assistant to a national committeeman at a national political convention. It was a great honor, and a second fellow was also the assistant since the committeeman's regular assistant had mistakenly promised the role to him as well. As we were leaving the convention one night, during a day where the negotiations had been particularly tough on a rules committee dispute with the presumptive national nominee, this other assistant started talking to reporters as the committeeman talked to reporters as well. I was standing in between them, was not committing this grievous error, and watched this trainwreck develop from the poorly-considered short answers to progressively longer "additions" to the comments by the committeeman. This glorified driver was giving quotes to reporters that were clearly erroneous, and clearly designed to give salacious nuggets about the nominee to the reporters. This kid was trying to get in the papers, and about to make serious long-lasting problems for this committeeman were he to be quoted.

As the three of us walked back to the hotel, I told him that he had to confess what he did, and finally told him that I was going to do it if he didn't. He eventually did, and I was sure that it meant the end for his budding political career. And, sure enough, the next day he was sent back to the office, but to my amazement he wasn't terminated. This clear and gross violation of protocol and bad decision-making was excused as rash youthful exuberance. People and managers can be a forgiving lot, if the problems don't fester and if they come with sincere regret and apology and a discussion of how to solve the problems.

But mark my words, you always want to be the first one to teacher. Which means that you can't get the same accommodation if others report the problem to your supervisor and then they have to confront you about it, or worse yet, they find out and don't confront you about it and let it fester. Confess mistakes and get these problems out of the way soon, don't try to solve them on your own, and don't involve others without the input of your supervisor.

Not involving coworkers might seem a bit extreme or paranoid. After all, they have the same experience and skill set as your boss in all likelihood. But all offices are small, word gets around, people love talking about drama and interesting developments, and your mistake will become known. And even if the water cooler discussions don't expose your mistake, be aware that almost every employer and likely every campaign reads emails, saves all emails received and sent, and also checks your phone logs. As a manager, it's simply too tempting to read them.

It's also too easy to archive them all, and the liability in not doing so is too great. Knowing who is talking to reporters and leaking information, knowing who is job shopping, the law is entirely on the side of the employer here, and one can set this up with the click of two switches on your email server that you'll never see. Every negative comment about your supervisors are going to be read, and when you discuss your mistakes with coworkers over email, it's also likely to be read. Be very careful about what you send out. Your personal email is more likely to be immune to their prying eyes, but is still easy to get access to if it gets sent across their computers or over their internet connection, so be aware and be careful. And never assume that a place isn't reading emails because they're nice or that those things are only done by places that don't trust their employees. There's no way to predict which place reads emails, and you should always assume and always act as if they're reading yours.

Although I've never done it, and the laws are a bit different involving phone calls, your employer can also likely listen in on your calls. That's a less likely concern, but it would be best to be disciplined about your comments and loose tongue about coworkers and especially your superiors. Don't joke or say things about them over email or the phone that you wouldn't say to them in person, or if they were listening, because in many cases they are.

The eighth piece of advice about how best to keep your job is to watch out for vendors. When you initially meet vendors, they seem like extra staff who are offsite. They're often a godsend, a way to get that mailing out on time or a group who is able to augment your performance while adding just a bit onto the bottom line. And, overall, they do function that way. But you, as an individual staffer, represent an implied threat to a vendor. Because there are vendors for every type of campaign function, every staff member is either a direct replacement of a potential vendor function or a siphon off of money that could go to a particular vendor's product.

Media vendors will tell you that all elections are decided in the media. Yard sign vendors will talk about name ID and how important they were to some specific mayor's election in a town you've never heard of. Website vendors will talk fancy to your campaign manager or vice president about social networking and the impact of "Millennials" on elections and peddle their snake oil. It's a wide wild world of political vendors, but you are not part of their profit margin.

They will seem like your friends, they will act like your friends, but they are not your friends.

Many vendors and consultants are former staffers or are connected in previous ways. Many have private or personal relationships with staffers and those in charge, and they do favors, just like anyone else in politics, to secure their position. They might donate a mailing to your nonprofit, or cleanup a list and charge a reduced rate, or have saved someone's neck a decade ago and be living off that kindness for many years. But again, these people view you as a direct threat to their profit margins.

Mail vendors, in particular, can often make their entire year's budget off of a very small number of campaigns if they are doing all the mail for that campaign. If they're living off 6 campaigns assuming that each does 12 serious mailings with them in a cycle, that's only 72 mailings from which to make their bottom line. If you recruit scores of volunteers, and donated printers and decide to do one of those on the cheap with free help, you just cost them a significant percentage of their total budget. You thought you were adding value to the campaign, you saved a ton of money and got volunteers involved, and everyone seems happy except for that mail vendor's kids who now won't get an Xbox for Christmas. You are eating into their bottom line, and while they might like you in the abstract, they don't consider you an asset.

As well, an entire consultant class exists to make their living by giving obvious or bad or obviously bad advice to campaigns. These people don't "work" as much as they furiously type emails, and your actions are a threat to their existence. They have spent years developing contacts and doing favors to get to this point, and your actions and educated opinions are threatening that sweet life.

I was called in to help turnaround a statewide referendum in the Midwest, and was having the hardest time getting anything serious done and couldn't figure out why. Even though I was from out of town, my recommendations so far to build an in-house phone bank, focusing volunteers on voter contact, identification, and lit dropping targeted precincts, seemed non-controversial. I was even more perplexed to hear the supervisor I reported to, the effective leader of the referendum, say that she wanted to do a major media push in a state that lacked serious media markets.

It took a few weeks for me to discover that the local party hack and consultant, based several states away, kept giving this woman the worst advice in the world. Pushing media over grassroots on a grassroots issue, he was lining his consultant pockets with the commissions on an issue funded by elderly grandmothers and their direct mail checks. It was shameful, and disgusting, but this consultant quickly saw me as a threat. What many people, even political veterans, either don't know or too soon forget is that consultants make most of their money on the 15 percent kickback they get from preferred vendors. So, this consultant directs all his clients to the same mail house that, in turn, kicks back to the consultant, a nice little network of profit, but a sure-fire way to bankrupt campaigns. This snake even had the audacity to claim that the vendors he was referring to were discounting all their rates by 15 percent, which seems like a deal until you realize that we had nothing to compare the original rates to, and that it still meant he was getting his commission in addition to a $5,000 a month retainer.

This consultant, almost single-handedly, made sure this statewide referendum lost. I left the campaign in order to avoid the impending trainwreck, but it was amazing to watch the destruction that these overpaid and underwhelming consultants can wreak on a campaign or organization. They are all so money-focused that they can't be trusted.

I wish I could say this was an isolated experience. A few years later, I was running a senate race involved with a consultant firm that was just as awful. These state-based consultants kept recommending major media buys to my candidate (notice a commonality here of consultants always advising what brings in money to them) and were generous enough to forego a retainer. They were planning to make it all up, of course, on the commissions later and by directing business to their vendor friends. The routine here isn't complicated, their motives quite transparent when one sees how they regularly operate, and understands their payment scheme. They recommended my candidate raise money, spend none, and blow it all on media, on a race that could only be won, if at all, on the grassroots. As they were shutting down a voter database, I realized that the cause was lost. There was even a point where I was in the room with all these "unpaid" consultants and the candidate where I realized that I was the only one there who actually wanted my candidate to win.

These guys aren't paid if they win, there's no money-back guarantee if they lose, and many of them are losers. The firm I just told you about hadn't been involved with a winning statewide race against an incumbent for 18 years at that point, so whatever advice they were giving, I was pretty confident it wasn't right simply by their track record. But there's no penalty in Consultantland for losing. They can suck time, money, and resources away on red herrings and dead ends because they are trusted by the candidate because "they're the professionals." These people are singularly motivated by money, and can never be fully trusted. They see you as a threat to their finances, and so they will never truly trust you and besides, you're not the candidate, so what do they care when they have access to the candidate. So many campaigns renege on their debts that perhaps they have to be that way, but whatever the rationalizations for their avarice, what matters to you is that they'll try to be your friends and at the same time be trying to undermine you so that the organization needs to hire them that much more after you're gone.

Vendors ought to always report to the member of the campaign that they're responsible to, which might seem obvious but never happens this way due to those long-term relationships they build up. What that means in practice, then, is that the fundraising mail vendor should be underneath, and report solely to, the fundraising director or chairman. The vendor for your internet service and website should report to your communications director or chairman, not to your organization's president or your candidate. To let vendors have a privileged relationship and have direct access circumventing your hierarchy and chain of command is to invite drama, debacles, and disaster later. It's also giving them an all-too-opportune chance to displace you in favor of their inferior service.

Just remember that the campaign will pay them first and you last. They'll charge $5k a month for advice via email, while you'll get pennies, and yet you'll be left holding the chair when the money-music stops. If you or your campaign insists on using them, just make sure to ask a few basic questions such as getting their references, finding out which races they've won, and which races they've won that were truly competitive.

Most races in politics are safe seats, someone getting anointed from within the party establishment and structure, and the overall exercise of "democracy" being a formality not too different from a Soviet election with one name on the ballot. Functionally, most elections, at all levels, only have one option on the ballot. These sure-fire election winners will still hire consultants, and those consultants will take credit for the victory. If you're involved with a serious race, you want someone who knows how to win, not someone who knows how to pick uncontested battles.

The cause and candidate in both elections with those two consultants I mentioned before lost, and lost by the same margins as they always lose, doing the same things they had always done, and will probably continue to do. I'm sure they either chalk it up as a great victory "considering the long odds" or don't even mention it when soliciting the next client.

Yeah, I don't like consultants.

One would be wise to be militant about the consultant relationship from the beginning, because to try and correct a bad or dysfunctional vendor relationship mid-stream, or on a campaign at the worst time possible, in September or October before a November election for example, is another surefire recipe for disaster. And when these liars are finally discovered to be liars, the election will be over, the checks will be cashed, and short political memories will fade by the time the next cycle comes around and this whole situation will repeat itself. Vendors belong well entrenched in your hierarchy, and are always in pursuit of the dollar. Consultants are wholesale liars who do no work and charge ridiculous rates for the same advice you could find in a book by Paul Wellstone about applied politics. Use vendors sparingly and avoid consultants.

The ninth best way to keep your job is to avoid workplace relationships. Even though it may seem like something natural, unexpected, or not affecting others, it does, always. These relationships hurt your position in the office, and almost always lead to drama and stress your boss.

Campaigns especially have this sort of latent sexual tension found among young people working long hours, around people they philosophically agree with, and in pursuit of a common dream. It's a recipe for relationships and it's natural. But, especially for campaigns, as much as possible, wait to have the relationship after election day. Frankly, it's better in general to stay single and focused on a campaign and then engage relationships after the election.

After all, the most precious and unmovable commodity for campaigns is time, and relationships take up an enormous amount of time. Even those that get confined to the after-work hours take hours of your evening away from other things you need to do to remain a productive worker during the day. Just putting them off for a few months until you get past the campaign is the ideal way to resolve this, and it's entirely doable.

I once had a coworker describe this idea and concept as "not shitting where you eat," a blunt and direct metaphor for an essential truth. Bringing relationships into the workplace is almost always problematic. Even outside the complications of dating your boss, an intern, or a vendor, workplace relationships are problematic even before getting into those hairy situations as well. The best option is just to put them off until after the election, you won't appreciate how much drama you avoid by doing this, but it is the right choice.

Another piece of related advice, that might seem a tad extreme, is to avoid getting a pet during a campaign. The lonely nights can seem less so if one has a dog or a small pet to keep one company, but it's a time and money sink as well. You'll be so busy and so preoccupied with getting election-related items finished that you'll easily forget to feed or neglect to give appropriate care and handling to a pet and risk its health. Again, I realize how crazy this seems, but no matter how busy your political job seems in the summer, multiply it by five and you'll approximate what September and October will feel like. Avoid the pets, and you'll save a few doggie lives in the process.

I mentioned it briefly before, but want to be clear that inter-hierarchy dating is almost always a disaster. It seems fine at the time, but the two things you have to consider is what happens when others see you in the relationship and perceive preferential treatment, real or imagined, and also what happens when the two of you eventually split. If your partner is a child of a major donor, perhaps that donation will dry up. Perhaps a sexual harassment suit will result, perhaps the office will split into factions, and the office dynamic could become entirely poisoned by whose series of events are more believed for the breakup. After all, almost no breakup occurs without anger and resentment by one party against the other, and introducing that element into an already chaotic political organization is asking for trouble.

Dating interns, made famous by Clinton and Lewinsky, might seem okay at the time but is, as well, almost always wrong. The job title "intern" has, since Clinton, become too attached to inappropriate relationships, and dating a campaign intern or even an organizational intern can be seen as very bad decision-making on your part. Date another organization's interns, but dating your own is going to be seen poorly by the rest of the office, it comes across as a very predatory move, and breeds resentment from women who look down on it and men who can often be jealous. And whatever the individual motives for resentment, it ultimately hurts your position to a great deal. If you're attending functions and getting out and about, find a good partner somewhere other than where you work, it's by far the best option.

There's also a need to say that workplace sex is a bad idea. It can seem hot at the time, and plenty of people have certainly been guilty of it, but the repercussions are disastrous, perhaps adding to its excitement. And realize that the first time you do it, someone will find out and everyone will know. I worked for one group and a very mousey man, a rather unassuming Casanova, was well-known for his sexual escapades on almost every desk in the office. I didn't know this fellow that well, but once one person found out, people couldn't stop talking about it. Another employee, someone closer to this author, had sex in the office and then fell asleep, awoken hours later by the rustling of employees coming into the office as the two lay naked nearby.

Outside of the salaciousness of the story, think about it practically. There's no explaining this, and there's no massaging your way out of this mistake to your boss. It's a clear demonstration of bad judgment, and will permanently and forever wreck your working relationships with the entire office, which will find out minutes after you're found out. It's a debacle you don't live down and, at best, only becomes the office joke and constant reference, something that will stunt your professional advancement, and the story can easily follow you to future workplaces. You won't think about this at the time, of course, you'll just be enthralled by the excitement of the experience, but avoid this problem by confining your sexual relations to places outside the office.

And in case you're curious, the two naked lovebirds in the office did manage to make a clean getaway, but don't let that be false encouragement, as they made a most disgraceful exit with their clothes in hand out a fire escape door onto the morning street of a city.

As a common note in all these stories, be very wary of kissing and telling. If you make any of these transgressions, keep them to yourself and try to remain discrete. Keep your personal drama out of the workplace, and if you can't avoid workplace relationships, certainly avoid workplace drama that accompanies such relationships as much as possible.

The tenth piece of advice would be to watch out for the family of the boss, the candidate, and the major players in your organization. Candidates' spouses, especially, come in two flavors. Either they are completely remote and detached from their spouse's political ambitions (think of Dr. Judith Dean, wife of Howard Dean who almost never hit the campaign trail) or the overinvolved and personally politically ambitious spouse who wants to be almost more involved than the candidate themselves. The underinvolved ones aren't a problem, because you can just treat them with respect and be considerate of their decision to avoid politics.

The ones who want to be overinvolved are another matter, though. It can be initially frustrating to feel like you have to work around them or that they serve as a second boss. But angering them is a guaranteed losing position. Essentially, these people want to help out, they've been around the candidate for a long time and feel as though they know them better than you ever could, and use that relationship to assume control. It's frankly going to be very difficult for you to convince these kinds of people that you know better than they do. In many cases, these people have been involved with your candidates from the very moment when their first election was conceived, and spend every day with them. You can't compete with that kind of influence.

These spouses want to help out, but too often helping out means calling all the shots. They might appreciate your input at first, but in time will likely see you as a competitor for the time and their personal agenda and ideas about how the campaign ought to be run. Additionally, they'll start looking down at you. It's a bad situation and position to get yourself into, and the best solution is avoiding it happening in the first place. If you find an overinvolved spouse, keep a very positive, cordial relationship and try to solve any problems right away. Certainly don't let things fester because they'll be able to wage a much better war of attrition against you than you can appreciate.

A good piece of advice here is to talk to people who have worked for your candidate or supervisor before, innocently ask them for advice on how to best succeed in your relationship with the spouse. Don't probe for gossip here, and don't engage in anything that can't be explained later if found out, so stay very respectful of the spouse even if you don't particularly care for them. Find out the best way to handle the spouse, and how to keep her happy. Remember that you aren't managing their relationship, as the candidate is always going to be married to the spouse or going out with the individual, but you can figure out ways to keep the spouse happy and ideally find out what particular things she enjoys the most.

Many younger spouses want to engage people in their demographic, they think that the key to electoral success is in winning over people just like them. Giving them clear authority and responsibility, and enabling, encouraging, and assisting them to reach the goals based off of their specific role is a good way to somewhat contain their involvement so that they don't become overinvolved in every decision. Overinvolved spouses, similar to overinvolved bosses in general, can become a real burden. Left unchecked, every small decision on the campaign will soon require their approval and insight, and decisions that seem resolved will get reopened repeatedly.

A campaign I was working on had this situation arise, and the most trivial of issues kept being revisited and debated, things I didn't even care about. The yard signs, the logo, and even the placement and fonts used in the logo were under constant scrutiny and attack. Remember that people who don't work in politics tend to overemphasize the things that really don't matter: the sexy glamorous things, the things they've seen in movies and heard from television.

Every woman I've ever met in politics was nuts about *The American President* with Michael Douglas and every guy had seen *Wag the Dog* at least twice. For whatever reason, those were the two movies that people based many of their preconceptions of politics upon. The truly good-hearted people in politics have all seen *Dave* with Kevin Kline, and no one has seen *The Distinguished Gentleman* with Eddie Murphy, though it's my favorite and you should watch it. Each of those is based on the presidency (except the *Distinguished Gentleman*), and none are really about campaigns. Spouses don't understand a voter file, voter contact, or the mechanics of fundraising, and those things are always boring to them. They want to believe that the campaign's success hinges on the effective design of yard signs, "messaging" and "branding," and the proper placement of those yard signs.

People watch these shows and then get ridiculous ideas about politics. They think that the big sentimental action at the end, at the last possible minute, wins elections. This is the product of political training via Hollywood. A hilarious example of this was a lobbying campaign that involved sending a certain color letter to the government to lobby them on a controversial issue. The organizers thought that the receipt of a lot of letters would cause the government to act. Anyone with experience in the mailroom in D.C. can tell you that color coding the trash just makes their job that much easier. Their hearts were pure, but they had been giving a false set of ideas, they thought that government worked like the movies, where people's hearts do a 180 when they see the passion of youngsters. Another hilarious example along the same lines was the Ron Paul blimp, financed with PAC money, to fly around broadcasting the name of the little-known Texas congressman's presidential campaign. The only problem is that renting a blimp is quite pricey, and the monthly bill was in the hundreds of thousands of dollars. It was an amazing, truly amazing, waste of money, on an almost colossal scale. But, again, people will come up with these kinds of ideas due to the cinematic experiences they've had which give them false notions about how people vote, and what it takes to win an election.

One potential permutation worth mentioning and considering here, as well, is the potential future career of the spouse. Even if it's unrealistic, it may be entirely probable and natural in the mind of the spouse. The candidate with the yard signs had a very long and ethic name that was hard to pronounce if one wasn't familiar with it, so campaign management 101 would say to use the candidate's friendly first name instead. What I didn't realize at the time, what I had failed to consider fully, was that the overinvolved spouse not only wanted to help win her husband's race, but also harbored future political aspirations of her own. Over the course of several months, this was only mentioned to me three times by two people, so even though I was in a position of trust, this was rarely directly stated. The use of the yard signs and the use of the last name in the logo would help grow the name identification for her future race.

I handled that situation poorly, and the right answer would have been to encourage the wife's involvement more, and give her the authority over those areas she took the most interest, and not contest her aesthetic decisions, no matter how much I disagreed with them or thought them ultimately counterproductive. Keeping a happy spouse keeps a happy candidate and keeps you with a paycheck and a job, a happy outcome at a small price. The more generalized cliché applicable here would be to not stop and fight every battle, and save your political capital for the major decisions instead.

Finding a good role for these valuable people can easily involve speaking engagements, very light fundraising items, networking, and those issues that are very subjective, such as the before-mentioned logo and signage questions. Those projects are practically designed for the overinvolved spouse.

Be alert if the overinvolved spouse suddenly becomes apathetic or seemingly disconnected from the campaign, be aware that this could be their frustrated withdrawal from the campaign and could signal that they're upset at you and that you ought to speak with the spouse and find a good way to reconnect them with the campaign. The overinvolved spouse will rarely simply give up on the campaign; despite their frustrations, they're in for the long haul. So act quickly upon sign that they're dissatisfied and bring them back into the campaign team.

I've spent a decent amount of time discussing the spouse, but the candidate's family is also worth considering. They are likely in business and have actual or perceived special skills. Specifically, a computer science major may want to run your website or voter database. This would be a major mistake and requires a certain delicacy to avoid and dismiss their offer for help. Good excuses here are the many laws and regulations involved with handling such data and the potential risks of protecting such data. You want a professional outfit to run vital aspects of your campaign. Also, there's a political liability in hiring family members because it will look bad to donors on filings and disclosures, and even if they take no pay it can still be considered a donation that you need to calculate. But the fundamental reason you don't want to do this is that you need the ability to fire these people if they make mistakes.

The data, the money, and the massive time involved in reconciling major problems with these systems make them necessary to be handled only by professionals. People who deal with corporate database systems are not easily transferable to political operations, even though people in business think they can do anything and the candidate's relatives naturally just want to help out. Keep the vital functions of the organization and campaign entrusted to professionals, people who aren't going to accidentally set the passwords to "password" or overlook a potential bug that deletes huge chunks of data or a major coding issue that results in your FEC filings getting turned in late and incurring significant fines. Family members are almost always amateur hour, and you can use their help on non-vital systems or to review and give suggestions on the professional actions by vendors. But don't trust them to run your vital systems or you'll get into serious problems that you can't get out of painlessly.

The next seven pieces of advice are tied to the advice elsewhere to keep focused on self-improvement, read new skill areas to round out the political technology you're exposed to, and increase your value as an employee by getting more skills.

The first skill to consider, and the eleventh piece of advice, is to get better at fundraising. Easily, one can learn the various types of fundraising, for political groups it's a small world of direct mail, direct solicitation, events, and telemarketing. There's also the world of online fundraising made successful by the insurgent Presidential campaigns of Howard Dean in 2004 and Ron Paul in 2008. From these types of fundraising, one can get more experience in any specific subset.

Political direct mail has an excellent book by Ben Hart, *Fund your cause with Direct Mail*, that can get you started on the basics and provide enough context to make you feel comfortable with the unique writing style and methods used in direct mail. Direct mail, known to most as "junk mail," is an art form with specific vendors and consultants in every state who can help write, print, and mail your letters. Where you can stand out is by understanding the whole mail process and contributing to the contents of the letters. Letters will be sent to two types of lists, prospect lists and to a donor file. Prospects are prospective donors, potential ones. The donor file is the list of those who reliably send money in. Stories and anecdotes are valuable for these letters, and little details can make the difference between a successful letter and an unsuccessful one, so collecting useful stories and providing them to your fundraising chairman can be a big benefit and help. You will be surprised at how poorly most people tell stories and how the fundraising letters don't match what's really going on with the campaign.

If you're alert and aware of what's going on, and excited about the things going on, and you have a powerful anecdote, make sure to share that with the fundraising chairman. A single-mother who donates her time to make sure her child has a better mayor, a retiree who has seen other politicians come and go and really believes in your candidate, a young high school student who just learned about local elections and wants to make a difference by helping out, are all the sort of stories that are quite easy to overlook or take for granted but could make for wonderful direct mail. The kinds of stories they need are the ones that most people just gloss over, unfortunately. Send along anything you think potentially useful for letters to the fundraising chairman as much of it will be useful, and this is a great way to get started with this kind of fundraising.

These letters are typically drafted or outlined by staff and then handed off to the regular vendor who handles the packages. Most outfits model their letters after the normal letters they see elsewhere, with a lot of bolding, italics, underlining, and exclamation points. These are the kind of letters that read as though someone is screaming at you. In reading Hart's book you'll quickly see that the best letters are the ones that pack a punch, tell good stories, and don't exaggerate or overstate their claims.

There's a whole world of resources to become a better writer at direct mail, and you can check those out. Understanding the entire process and how to take a Microsoft Word document, properly combine it with an excel list, and successfully merge those into a mailing, print it, correlate it with the right addresses, and successfully get it into the mail is a real skill set; it's something you only learn through a lot of mistakes and lots of trial and error. The post office, as frustrating as they are, also requires that mail delivered in bulk be sorted by what's known as the "Area Distribution Code" when it comes to them. If you're sending mail all to a very small geographic area this isn't as necessary as if you're sending across state lines, nationally, or across a state. The easiest method is to get software to generate these ADC codes on your mailing labels, but be aware that getting mail to your donors, supporters, and potential donors isn't as simple as just printing a letter and giving it to the post office; it's a definite skill set and being good at it and being familiar with it will make you considerably more valuable as an employee.

Getting better at direct solicitation, asking people for donations in person, requires considerably more gusto. People are often uncomfortable with asking others for money, even though there's no reason to have any trepidation about it. You can become better at asking people for money in person through experience, and also understanding human nature better, and the many reasons why people donate money. There's another good book relevant here, *Asking* by Jerold Panas, that outlines the ways to overcome your natural anxiety for asking people for large amounts of money. Specifically, the book discusses four primary objections that people have to donating that is extremely useful. The four objections are the timing of the gift, the institution, the project, or the amount. Giving proper context to these objections and the easy ways to engage and deal with the objections, you read and learn quickly good ways to work with potential donors to maximize their giving to worthy causes. The book is wonderfully written and a quick read.

Many people on campaigns ask for money and they're used to doing it, but small objections and problems can get overblown. Have a cool head to offer some friendly advice, based on what Panas says, as well as the many other books about personal fundraising. You will also need to track your individual prospects and meetings with these individuals, and do the proper follow-up in order to secure the gift and make sure the promise or pledge to give actually comes in. It also helps to have strong research skills here, to learn as much about potential donors before you make a financial request, so you have a better idea of what they're interested in, and what's likely to be appealing to them.

Event fundraising is similar to direct solicitation, except that you gather those potential donors together and then get their financial involvement in various ways. Events can have an admission fee to get to the event, as is done with pricey per-plate dinners with the candidate, or housewarming parties where the host goes to each of his guests and gets them to invest. Event fundraising can be a prominent speaker who comes and gives a presentation that ends with a request for funds, and it can be in a large auditorium or in a small gathering in a house. Events come in all shapes and sizes, and there's really no "wrong" type of event for a candidate or an organization, there's just always the very strong risk that the event won't be profitable.

These kinds of events can be unpredictable in their costs and also in their attendance. Good events are those ones where every potential problem has been thought out in advance and contingencies considered. The best type of person for this kind of role is an event planner, or someone with wedding planning experience. These kinds of people can be hard to deal with, though, so keep that in mind. Constantly overworked, or perceiving themselves as overworked, those working on event planning for your campaign or candidate can always use another pair of reliable, hardworking hands. This area of fundraising is a great place to learn, and easy to get the experience as the help is always needed.

Another kind of fundraising, the type that most want to hate, is telemarketing. It's painful, agonizing, and grueling, and it works every time. Many campaigns outsource this to a vendor, and in doing so lose money they need elsewhere and sacrifice a considerable amount of quality control.

Phone lines are cheap, and setting up a phone bank can be done relatively easily. If your campaign doesn't have one, start sketching out how to make one and show some initiative.

I don't have a specific book to recommend here, but I'm sure there are plenty out there if you searched Amazon. The eight basic things you need to construct a phone bank are the:

1) Physical space
2) Phone lines
3) Equipment
4) List
5) Call list (printed)
6) Script
7) Volunteers
8) Mail/process for follow-up on pledges

The process for dialing for dollars and dialing for votes is not much different, except that the scripts vary. Gathering a dozen volunteers to make calls for a few hours a week to start is how most phone banks start. And once people get used to making the calls, it gets much easier over time. But keep people together, phoning for votes or dollars all by yourself is a depressing and futile enterprise, and the burnout rate is much, much higher than if done in a small group. Recruit young voices to light up your lines, and retirees are also known to make good phoners. You get good through experience, and your campaign or organization becomes good at in-house telemarketing through experience as well. You'll soon see what works, especially if you're diligently tracking the numbers of calls made, bad numbers, pledges, and assessing those statistics. This is a great way to add value to yourself and to the organization, and really let your leadership shine.

The last type of fundraising to consider is online fundraising. In an age where the laws have greatly curtailed the use and resell of email lists, it's increasingly difficult to raise money through online sources, and though Howard Dean, Ron Paul, and Barack Obama have had great success, each represented very unique circumstances as well. The one thing that seems to work the best is having an easy-to-use donation page and donation widgets for your website to capitalize on moments of high traffic for earned media and when your organization gets wide notice and exposure. Many vendors and consultants will greatly overpromise performance on online fundraising, but its wider application doesn't seem to have been fully realized for campaigns large and small, federal, state, and local. So have a site setup, and if your group lacks an online fundraising method offer to set one up, and figure out ways to drive potential donors to your site so that they naturally donate. Take the actions needed to drive the web traffic, and get the stories in the media that results in the kind of digital attention that naturally produces online donations.

As well, online web donation systems can be used to process telemarketing donations. So a good phone bank operation, mentioned before, can streamline their paperwork by having the phoner input the information through their donation portal. I also feel obliged to mention that, despite one's initial inclination, Paypal is notoriously difficult, onerous, and extremely frustrating to work with to process donations. Consider yourself warned.

The twelfth item to consider in ways to keep your job and a way to improve your value to the organization is to get better at technology issues. The problems most campaigns and groups run into are relatively simple and straightforward.

The simplest things to solve are the problems most people have with their individual computers, which often end up being the most personally aggravating issues to the people, and your solution can ingratiate you to them the most. The problems I've seen most regularly are those things that make a computer slow, with frustrated politicos yelling that their internet browsers aren't working fast enough.

First off, delete Microsoft's Internet Explorer and shift to a browser that actually works, like Mozilla's Firefox or Google's Chrome. Second, run and install programs that will detect spyware, viruses, and other similar issues. A nice trifecta of AdAware, Spybot, and Avast for viruses. Run these and solve any issues that come up just through a good Google search on how to remove troublesome programs. Also, run a simple disk defragmentation program at night and it will clear up a lot of the problems with the computer "running too slow." You'll find that this simple advice will clear up quite a few problems.

As preventative measures, make sure that your office is doing four things regularly: 1) resetting passwords and using real ones, 2) using power strips, 3) backing up your data somewhere secure, and 4) automating the windows updates and security patches. Almost every campaign starting out will overlook these issues, even though the cost on all of these things is virtually nothing.

Beyond the individual computers and the minor preventative measures you can deploy, setting up a simple secure wireless network and making sure you have an internet connection to the office is simple enough to do, and even if you don't know you can find out easily from Google. The other technology issues that regularly come up are things that are software specific and generic web issues involving the website.

If you want to become better with web issues, go to Godaddy.com and start your own personal website. You'll quickly learn through trial and error how to post pages and the simple HTML code. Make a goal to display your writing and pictures, and go from there. It won't be a skill you pick up overnight, but it's much easier than one thinks initially.

For software issues, almost every major program has clear tutorials on Youtube that you can watch and become a pro overnight, and the various web issues can also be solved through Google searches, Youtube tutorials, and a quick Craigslist ad asking for help, or finding a local technology guru who can help you solve simple problems. Some basic software systems, such as Dreamweaver for websites or Photoshop for graphics, can make a large difference for a campaign as well, especially the local ones who can't afford narrow specialty vendors.

Being versed in these simple solutions to problems will quickly make you an invaluable asset around the office. Truly, 90 percent of problems revolve around these issues and can be solved with many of these simple solutions.

The thirteenth piece of advice on how to best keep your job is to enhance your skills at event planning. This is often overlooked as a campaign skill because people take it for granted, but good events send a strong message to potential voters, the media and donors that your group is a professional outfit and are winners. The best experience for this, as I said before, is through wedding planning and leading similar events.

Host a social event, and invite a large number of people. Make a list of all the associated things that have to happen, and the things you need to do to ensure turnout. A simple barbecue at your house can easily become complicated if you change the number of invitees from 10 to 60 and introduce the element of asking people to contribute towards the food. These are the exact situations you'll find yourself in during the campaign, having to plan social events on the fly, needing to collect money, and trying to figure out how to get people to actually attend the event.

Many communities also have summer festivals that you can help out at and get a taste of what it takes to put together a major event. Many social orders, fraternal societies, and local organizations have events that can be useful to volunteer with as well. You may not have considered how that upcoming Kiwanis pancake breakfast was useful to your political career, but helping them to plan, execute, recruit volunteers, turnout people to the event, and also handle the transactions is great experience.

You want to learn how to be good at covering all the details, making lists, checking them twice, and dealing with seemingly unpredictable situations.

The fourteenth aspect of self improvement that will help you keep your job is to get better at data and statistics. This is a challenge, and though it's not a skill that you easily pick up, an increased familiarity with issues, concerns, and aspects of statistics will help you rise through the ranks. Statistics are vital for looking at voting patterns, predicting turnout, reading polls accurately, and determining where is the best place to put your few resources.

There are a variety of software platforms that you can use to work with this data. If you have your data held by a vendor, you may want to ask them which one will work best with your data. Many times, that just means using simple Microsoft Excel for your underfunded or basic campaign. Backing up your data, especially your spreadsheets, is also critical because it is perhaps the most common Excel mistake to resort the rows and lose the order of the data permanently, and when you're dealing with thousands of names, that's not a mistake easily corrected, hence the need for regular and serious backups, even if it's just to a flash drive.

The main issues are collecting the data, organizing the data, and using the data. Getting the best data set in the world is useless if you can't use it to generate a walk list to do a literature drop in a specific neighborhood. Both major political parties have voter databases that can be used, but sometimes getting access to this data can be difficult, and rarely given prior to being the official party nominee after the primary.

Know how to use the data, and how to generate a walk list. Even if someone else knows how, learn and become a backup. Another skill like this is getting up-to-date information from your state's Secretary of State office or the county clerk. Information about new voters registered in the area, historical voting data, and also those registering for absentee ballots are often easily obtained if you know how to get to this data. Learning this skill, as well, will be valuable in every political campaign you're involved with in the future.

Campaigns and all political organizations are highly reliant on effective data and up-to-date data; learning how to import new lists, acquire new lists and build your own lists can be very valuable. Finding ways to add, or what's called "append" data such as phone numbers is also a valuable skill to work with existing data. Adding and checking phone numbers can be done name by name, manually, with a website like Whitepages.com, or by sending your data to a vendor who can add those phone numbers to your list and then send it back to you, usually for a per-name matched fee.

Good campaigns rely on good data, so that they can avoid wasting their resources on reliable voters and spend their time identifying, contacting, and persuading the swing voters and also enhancing the turnout of their base voters.

The fifteenth way to keep your job is to get better at writing. Everyone thinks they're excellent writers, and people rarely admit that they need to improve. In reality, even the best writers need to constantly work on improving their abilities. Similar to much of the other advice, it's a skill honed through constant practice and exercise. This task can be difficult because getting good feedback is almost impossible. People are very well-conditioned to not give real feedback and will only give positive feedback. Find an English major or an English teacher to correct your grammar; encourage people who you know give brutal feedback to dissect your writing. It will sting and hurt quite a bit, but it will help improve your writing.

There are a wide variety of style books as well, but none surpass Strunk and White's classic *Elements of Style*, which is fabulous. Get it, read it, and then read it again. Another good classic is *Eats, Shoots and Leaves* by Lynne Truss. It's easy to fall into a trap of bad grammar, sloppy instant messaging and texting speech, which has broken sloppy thoughts, 1st grade vocabulary, and lacks eloquence. One way to break the bad habits our culture instills in our writing is to read great writers. High-minded magazines, for one, usually pride themselves on great writing. Your writing will become a reflection of what you read. In sum, you need to learn to be a better writer, practice becoming better, immerse yourself with great writing that you regularly read, and get the kind of feedback on your own writing that will allow you to become great.

Writing for pay, as a columnist, is also a viable option to become good quickly. A friend followed this path, recommended by a boss to a local newspaper, and it became a steady stream at $50 per column to write about politics, side income that helped and was a joy for him to write. Under pressure and under deadline is what separates the good from the great, and forces you to improve. Anyone can write great pieces if they have all the time in the world, but doing it regularly under pressure and under deadline is quite another thing. Get a basic book on grammar and leave it somewhere that you can go over easily. Try to read books on grammar when you get a moment.

The trick to good grammar is to keep your sentences simple. Call this the Hemingway approach to writing. It works well. Keep your thoughts direct and plain, and build from there. It helps to know the types of writing are typically used in politics.

Primarily, campaigns need press releases and very simple pieces for public consumption. Most campaigns want to pre-write letters to the editor to give to their supporters around the district and send in as their own. Campaigns also need legions of people to patrol blogs and comment boards to make sure they're sufficiently favorable to the candidate and toe the party line. There's also a need for webpage content, and updating existing information and putting out new stories, profiles, and items of interest. All of this writing, you can likely tell, is written at the lowest level possible so as to not be patronizing, with small words, simple ideas over subtle ones, and a total lack of nuance. The public thinks it wants Shakespeare, but it really prefers the comics, unfortunately. So, campaigns don't write to impress English teachers, they write to communicate basic ideas without controversy.

---

90 second primer on **Codewords**

Words are powerful, even in subtle almost subconscious ways they can "**frame**" an issue and influence the 35-40 percent of so-called "swing," independent voters. It's often fun to use **loaded language** to discuss your own positions in private, but in public you always have to stay "on **message**" and use the right **codewords**. No one lays these out for you, or makes clear that there are very definite right ways to talk about certain topics in politics and very wrong ways to talk about politics.

Overall:

Blacks are either **African-Americans** or just generally "**minorities.**" Directly describing a racial group is seen as either uncouth or unseemly. You also never directly define a type of employee by their **gender**. So you would never talk about a "stewardess" or "waitresses," you would refer to them as "flight attendants" and "wait staff."

Regardless of your political orientation, language is very tightly controlled to do the least offense possible, and that usually

means a very rigid adherence to the norms of what's called **political correctness**. It's also very politically fashionable to be on the cutting edge of new perceived offenses and to be as language-inoffensive/neutral as possible. Another example is to never refer to something as "retarded," even in the juvenile put-down way, as it would offend the mentally disadvantaged.

Right:

Abortion opponents are always referred to as "**pro-life**," abortion-rights supporters are "**pro-abortion.**" The particular abortion procedure called "**partial-birth**" abortion is described as such.

> Those against **gay marriage** are "**pro-family,**" those supporting it are supporting the "**gay agenda.**" Those favoring rules on unions are "**right to work.**" Those favoring immigration restrictions are for "**border security,**" "**immigration control,**" or "**border control**"
>
> Left:
>
> Abortion opponents are always "**anti-choice,**" supporters are "**pro-choice.**" Those against gay marriage are "**anti-gay extremists**" or "**homophobes.**" Those favoring rules on **unions** are "**anti-worker.**" **Immigration** opponents are "**nativists,**""**isolationists,**" or "**anti-immigrant**"
>
> In general, people you don't agree with are anti-something good and your side is pro-something good. You never give the opposition the benefit of the rhetorical doubt. The dry academic way in which one becomes accustomed to discussing issues and ideas in college gets cut away for the blood-sport of ideological politics, especially on the social issues. Don't get caught using the wrong language for your side or you'll stand out.

Political organizations and legislative offices have more of a need for stories, and currently many are poorly written. Some of this is due to a bias against any sort of creative writing, as well as stodgy editors, but if you want to deploy better writing skills, those are the right venues to do so. Becoming a better writer, though, is useful on campaigns to communicate simplicity, to become a veritable minimalist in your writing, packing the most punch in the shortest length.

Government offices, for what it's worth, are perhaps the most conservative in their writing and thus the least creative and most dry. They write to avoid controversy more than anything; their work is not designed to actually be read. Being a better writer is likely a luxury in a government office, and unrelated to your path to get ahead. Each type of employer, though, has a unique and specific style you want to learn and mimic as each has certain nuances to appreciate.

Writing practice, of course, makes perfect. So signing up as a writer, contributor, or reporter for a local statewide blog or web magazine is a good way to get regular assignments and also a small audience to critique your reporting and writing. Attending selected events as a reporter, asking a few questions, and writing up what you've discovered is a good way to do this. You can even make your own reporter's media credential to feel legitimate and pass any screening or security. I wanted to attend a political function in New Orleans, didn't want to pay the admission cost, and wanted to write a few stories about it, so I called up a few editor friends, said I would freelance to them for free, went and spent $1.25 laminating my press pass I made on Photoshop, and got in without any problems. Be assertive, aggressive, and creative, and you can get the experience you need quite easily to get paid to do this kind of work.

The sixteenth way to do better at keeping your job is to get better at being on the phone. It's something no one likes. My first job was as a credit card telemarketer, which I wasn't half bad at, and yet I still hate telemarketing. There's something about bothering people, typically over the dinner hour, which even sociopaths find rude and obnoxious. This is one skill that sitting down and practicing won't improve, because your mind will find ways to get out of doing the dialing.

After setting up phone banks in many different states in many different circumstances, I have yet to see people push themselves to actually make the calls.

What you need to do is to take everything you need to make the calls, find one or two other people to do this with, and for all of you to just lock yourself in a room and make the calls until you are finished. No amount of discipline will be sufficient to make the calls if your mind can find a way out of making them, so create an environment that you can't escape. This discipline even includes practicing the phoning, possessing a clear goal, and having someone else in the room to create the peer pressure to get your calls done and not leave before they're finished.

A good goal for a practice is to make 100 calls, hoping to get 10 of them to give an average of $20 each, for a total of $200 raised. This should take you about two hours or so to do, including many voicemails and wrong numbers. These goals might seem ambitious, but you can do it, and you'll run into a series of bad numbers of people who don't give and then get a few givers right in a row. It's not a steady pace, but stay disciplined and it will work out. The hardest part is to keep dialing the numbers. Each number will seem like you can feel physical pain as you push them, but keep chipper and remember that you're giving people a great opportunity to get involved with your project.

It's also important that if you become a phone bank manager that you stick with it and don't try to escape the pain of telemarketing. Stick with it. At one political nonprofit I was running, we created an intern phone bank at night that called prospective donors. To say that the interns hated this was an understatement, they were quite vocal in their great displeasure with this, yet they did amazingly well. There were nights they didn't raise a dollar in pledges, but there were days that we got $1,000 individual checks in the mail as a result of their calls. It was truly amazing to see what young, vibrant voices could do when effectively communicating a positive message. The tradeoff was that, even though I was the head honcho and was ostensibly "above" those calls, I needed to make them on my own both to make sure I always respected their work and also to show them that no one was above the grunt work.

Telemarketing never gets easy and never becomes pleasant. Even when you get good at it, it always seems like a painful chore. Stick with it, though, and encourage others to do so as well; you'll have great things happen for you and your group if you do it and do it well, and there's a lot of money and many votes that are just a phone call away. Getting good at phoning and understanding how to do it and make it work can make you a serious asset to any campaign or organization.

The seventeenth, and last point, about keeping your job through self-improvement is to get better at public speaking. This piece of advice might seem odd given that there are so few opportunities for public speaking, and it seems like it's a skill that won't be useful for years to an entry-level staff member. While there is some truth to that, becoming a better public speaker makes you a better person and a stronger presence. Becoming a better public speaker requires a serious amount of self-introspection and attention to exactly how you come across.

Perhaps the hardest part of being a better public speaker is, like becoming a better writer, getting good and honest feedback. Everyone in politics thinks they are a great speaker, because they never have the chance to see themselves speak. It's incredibly hard to improve by yourself, or using that awful old advice to practice in the mirror.

You want to start by identifying and understanding the real terms of public speaking, most people know what projection, diction, enunciation, and pitch is in the abstract, but often don't understand what it means in practice, or couldn't describe it in a given speech. Research the terms and understand what the points of critique are first. Then, search online for a few classic great speeches to mimic. There are some classic speakers and speeches that are easy to use, such as anything from Churchill, or major passages from Shakespeare. You don't need more than about five minutes worth of spoken material, either. Take this excerpt of a great speech and present it for someone to review. Are you able to project across a room, can you throw your voice at someone to get their attention across an auditorium, without a microphone and without yelling? It's a challenge even for great speakers.

Consider the appropriate emotion for a specific piece. Can you capture the subtle moral righteousness of Mario Cuomo's rebuttal to President Reagan during the 1984 Democratic Convention keynote? Get a few people to listen to you try this, and ask them to take notes on whether you did well on a main speaking issue you were working on, and also to rate you on a variety of terms that I just discussed. Perhaps you think you need to be more emotive in your speeches but you really have a pronunciation issue and you're mumbling your way through a presentation. As I said, it's extremely difficult to properly self-diagnose these issues, so you want to get good feedback and useful criticism from others.

The best way to improve, though, and I must admit that I take much of this advice from an incredibly brilliant public speaking coach that I had the pleasure of working with for several years in D.C., is to videotape your own speech and watch it. You will never find a harsher critic than yourself. The most common reaction I have seen from people is an absolute recoil at the mistakes made and such a cutting analysis, seeing every misstep and every minor mistake. Write all this down and review it; reflect and consider how to improve.

Work on one area of improvement at a time, you won't go from George W. Bush verbal fumbles to Barack Obama eloquence overnight, but you can improve very quickly if you can understand what you're really talking about, honestly assess and diagnose issues, and work on continued improvement in those specific areas. Common mistakes I have seen are speaking too quickly and not being able to fill a room with one's voice. Those are two very basic speaking skills and easy to work on. When you become skilled at mastering those two things, as well, you will see a noticeably different reaction from those around you if you use these new skills in daily life.

Those who speak slowly but intelligently are taken more seriously and considered more intelligent, less rushed, and more confident. Speakers who can fill a room can get someone's attention quickly and establish an interpersonal position of dominance by adjusting their volume to be just a tad louder than normal in social situations. That sounds like trickery or chicanery, but it's basic rhetoric that has existed since at least Ancient Greece. You owe it to yourself, and your political career, to become a better communicator for yourself and your principles.

Though you shouldn't worry about writing your own speeches, there are a variety of good speechwriting books out there. You shouldn't worry about it because there are plenty of good writers out there, and, frankly, there are few occasions to really use this skill in a structured way such as a public speech. However, Peggy Noonan, a Reagan speechwriter who wrote some of his best speeches, such as the national address after the Challenger space shuttle disaster, wrote *On Speaking Well*, which covers the subject very well. The main goal for you in becoming a better speaker is to have complete control and command over your presence so as to command respect.

Your presence is a tough thing to acknowledge and appreciate, and this kind of training can be tough to go through. You're forcibly changing yourself in a short period, and it isn't always easy. I don't want to pretend like it is. Many people have spent their entire lives living a certain way, such as always being timid, always doing what they were told, or never telling others what to do.

I've given public speaking workshops to college students in many states, and often volunteered to be an assistant debate coach wherever I was located, in addition to doing debate and forensics personally for many years. Through that experience, I have seen people change radically in short periods of time. I have seen timid girls become lions, and I've watched sloppy, messy people without ambition take the basic lessons of public speaking to heart and become sharp and focused and act upon the natural ambition that was always there. This change, though, can be disorienting.

One workshop in particular, sticks out. I was in Waco, Texas at Baylor giving a workshop where almost no one showed up. I was somewhat strung out from the road, doing this workshop as a favor to a group that asked because I was on their board and had a friend and political activist stowaway with me. As we went through the speaking workshop, though, I noticed that one of the few attendees was a timid girl who was just yearning to break out. We went through the ideas, the application, and then I asked her to stand up and confront the other people in the room, presuming them to be political adversaries and to be heated with them.

She did great, for about the first 90 seconds. And then the tears came. She cried, pouring out what seemed like a small lake of tears, and wouldn't stop. Psychologically, of course, we were forcing her way out of her comfort zone and her emotional response to this discomfort was pain and negative emotions. It was emotionally overwhelming for her, and boy did she let it show. What was even more interesting was that the side of her that understood what we were doing wanted to continue, and seemed appreciative of what was going on. Rarely have I been caught speechless and completely dumbfounded, but this was one such moment ... I wasn't sure whether to apologize, offer tissues, or keep going.

Future emails didn't get a response, though she did go to dinner with us afterwards, so I'm not sure what to make of my decision to do a little of all three options, but ultimately I know that it was the right decision to make because self-improvement is a messy path to actualizing our potential. As you go through these things and find discomfort in the frustration of learning something new, in the confusion of not always knowing what the right answer is, and in the likely alienation of previous friends who don't share your passion, realize that those are the natural consequences and byproducts of a process of self-improvement that you're going through. That process is very obvious and direct with public speaking, but exists in every decision you make to change a part of yourself in the fashion I've described.

It's tough, but it's worth doing, and later you won't regret it.

ACTION STEPS:

    1. Write out your tasks and goals

    2. Keep a time sheet

    3. Make a plan to reach work goals

    4. Make a plan to reach your career goals

    5. Keep your immediate task in front of you

    6. Control your performance to be good but not earth-shattering

    7. List out your deficiencies and solutions, get into a culture of self-improvement

    8. Get a list of all the training and networking events, and attend as many as possible.

Chapter 7. Getting Fired and Bouncing Back

It's an unpleasant thought, and an unpleasant reality: you are much more likely to get fired (or pushed to resign or forced out in some other way) from a political job than normal ones. Political jobs are unlike business jobs, and the office politics, the intense pressures, and the unrealistic demands will eventually get you. The best thing to keep in mind is to not fear its occurrence, and make yourself as ready as you can be for when it does happen.

Prepare yourself from day one to get fired from a job. Primarily, this means always having an up-to-date resume ready. It takes so little time to do this, but makes such a difference when you need it, and to have it ready to shoot off at a moment's notice. Your resume, after all, is just a method to getting a job interview, and you want to be ready to move into interview mode at the drop of a hat.

Keeping all your contacts backed up on your own drive or in your personal email is critical as well. Everything at your desk and everything on a company laptop can be gone in a moment, and they'll be under zero obligation to give you access to it later, so plan for the worst by making sure you have these things backed up. One thing that often comes up, especially among new staffers, is whether they should store and backup proprietary information, namely donor databases, of their workplaces. This is unbelievably foolish.

The thinking might be that this is your path to being a rich and famous consultant, but it's not. Not only can most places tell when you do this if they have a halfway competent tech person around, but it's very hairy for you later. If a future employer found this out, or if someone later learned that you were passing around old databases, that makes you look ridiculously untrustworthy, a blow to your reputation that can never be recovered. And, frankly, it's not worth it. Many databases have scores of outdated information and the lists are often full of people who donate to that particular organization alone. Their relationship is with that group or with that candidate, and so you'll be starting from scratch anyway.

So, the short of it is, don't waste your time, avoid the potential legal liability, and—most importantly—protect your good name by not stealing data from your employer. Instead, back up the kind of emails and contacts that are your own and that you'll need to be successful elsewhere, especially major reports, projects, or items that you worked on. Keep a record of your success, that's always something valuable to show others later and a potential source of items to add to your portfolio. Also keep the phone numbers and emails of key people you will need later.

When the firing, forced resignation, or termination happens, you're going to go through a very normal set of emotions. You'll get angry, confused, and depressed. The various stages of grief will set in, and part of it, when it happens, will just be letting time and distance take their natural course. But, initially, get your mind off work. If you're working a political job, you likely were 100 percent invested in the job and are losing not only your job but your social network as well; it's a very traumatic experience all around.

Take a moment to write out your accomplishments, the things that you're very proud of, and send an email to yourself highlighting these things. This email will come in handy later when you're talking about this job to others. And then do something that gets your mind completely off politics or the job. Do something mindless, indulge your hobbies for a day, and focus on staying happy and considering your next opportunity. You don't have a scarlet "f" tattooed on you because you get fired, even though it might seem like it. There are likely scores of great opportunities awaiting you, but take some personal time to reflect. I knew someone in D.C. who was terminated in the morning and by the afternoon had another job lined up and was at that next job the next day. That's a reflection of someone who took the next offer and probably didn't stop to consider the full range of possibilities he had in front of him. It would feel good to have that next job so quickly, as a kind of shot in the arm of personal self-worth, but the smart money is on getting several offers and weighing those carefully.

After all, what do you really want in a job? There are many things you can't avoid: work will always take effort, require some clinched smiles, and involve dealing with B.S. But what's really best for you is a question worth asking and answering here. Most importantly, what caused the firing and how can you avoid this at the next workplace? As I said, the temptation is to view this as a major failure on your part, but you'd be shocked to learn how many people in D.C. have been fired at one point or another. In many ways, it's just the nature of the beast.

But, when the firing happens, and it most likely will happen, resist the temptation to take drastic action immediately afterwards. I knew a girl who was fired from an entry-level position in D.C. and had her boyfriend drive out from the Midwest the very next day. She was leaving town, never to return. And you're probably thinking that's crazy, and I would never do that. And I might agree with you, if I didn't pull the same maneuver about five months after she did. It's just too tempting in that situation. Your pride is hurt, your emotions are scattered over the floor and you're confused, angry and drastic action seems like the only solution.

It's not. Patience and endurance are the virtues to keep in mind in moments like this, as well as a healthy perspective and realization that these things happen all too often.

The only way to stop a firing is to prevent it in the first place. And when you consider that it's an eventuality, you can finally come to grips with it and start taking active steps to avoid it and leave on your own terms.

One should always appreciate how frequent it happens, though; otherwise you get lulled into a false sense of security in political jobs that will ultimately make yours the next head on the chopping block.

Most managers hate firings. They're uncomfortable moments; there's a huge cost to the company; there's enormous legal liabilities involved; and there's never the right words to use. Just the turnover costs and hassle of finding a new employee makes it a mess.

Your boss, even if he's acting strange or hostile towards you, doesn't want to roll the dice on a new employee. If you haven't been fired yet, there's always a chance to turn it around, and a way for you to keep your job.

Fundamentally, most terminations involve some level of miscommunication, in that expectations aren't clear or properly understood, or the superior isn't communicating dissatisfaction with some element of the work performed. In political jobs, everyone is often worked to the bone, and so there's no real time for what "management" should be (getting the most out of people and facilitating their heightened performance and full potential), but rather your bosses likely have their own work to do in addition to making sure you get done with yours.

If you feel as though your work is getting to the point where a termination might be coming soon, have you spoken with your boss about your work performance and really gotten a full airing of grievances? This requires some delicacy, as many people dislike confrontation so they might be too accommodating in person, but really have unstated resentments.

I had a political job with a nonprofit and started prepping my resume and getting ready to get fired, even though by the numbers everything was great. My boss, who worked offsite, was extremely curt and hostile towards me. So, I asked for a six month review, in writing. She happily obliged, and only there did I learn that my bad habit of coming in late was making her quite upset. She voiced this, but I had overlooked it because she was offsite and I figured that she didn't care; others came in late, and I regularly stayed at the office so late into the evenings that I figured it didn't matter what time I arrived in the morning. But it did, and that review helped me make a point to come in at the time we agreed on and to make clearer to her the times I was staying late.

It seemed petty to me at the time because I wanted to be judged by my work product, and not a timecard. But she was the boss and I was the underling. I had to make her happy, and this was the cost of doing that. It took a setting and situation where she didn't have to be confrontational (she could just write this stuff out) for her to communicate what she thought I was doing wrong. That's one classic mistake I had made in the past, and seen plenty of others make as well: they accepted what was said as reality, forgetting the many social pressures bosses feel when someone comes to them in that setting. They don't want a fight, but they want their desires and expectations met as well. So they often don't verbalize what they want, get upset to the point of a firing, and everyone can't figure out later what happened.

If your boss is not being clear, ask her to write out a review of you and your work so you can make efforts to improve. Then really take to heart what she writes. And since political jobs are so transient and there are often plenty of people vying for your spot, do whatever your boss says. If he hates nose rings, take out the nose ring. You might start screaming about your constitutional right to a nose ring, but it won't matter. You'll end up with a pink slip and wish you had just avoided this mess by easing your boss's particular pet peeve.

You always want to nip these things in the bud before they grow into termination hearings.

When the firing happens, and you have some kind of termination hearing or meeting, realize that at that point it's over. Any rebuttal or argument will fall on deaf ears. They've made their decision, it's unpleasant and no one likes it, but it's the way things are, and it won't change. If you feel compelled to explain yourself, go ahead, but it won't change anything. You can't talk your way out of it by the time they come to fire you.

The best thing you can do for yourself, and perhaps the classiest option, is to thank them for the opportunities that the job gave, say you're sorry that it didn't work out, wish them all the best, shake hands, and leave. I've left positions with grace and I've left them with a verbal manifesto of their wrongdoings, and I can say that you'll always be more proud of the times you were graceful in defeat. I was once terminated from a job where I was the only employee, under the worst of circumstances, as they were deciding to refuse thousands of dollars of reimbursements, and they brought in an outside human resources manager to supervise the situation. It was ridiculous. But, despite all that, I was pleasant and let them make their decision, and wished them the best.

There's simply no point in being ugly about it, and why give them the satisfaction of later saying how nasty you were on the way out? Go out with class. As the officers said to one another to retain their composure and fortitude as the Titanic was sinking, "Be British."

Depending on who fires you, there may also be the chance to appeal their decision to another authority, perhaps the candidate, the nonprofit president, or a board of trustees. This is an unqualified mistake as well. Because there's no way to successfully make this appeal, and no way to make it look like it's not just bad feelings and personal animosity. I was running a nonprofit and during two firings, months apart, both employees tried this trick with me and came to me about the manager who fired them. I listened to them, and thanked them, but I still wasn't going to undo what had already happened.

I didn't undo this for two main reasons: First, the chain of command, which sounds very detached and dispassionate, and perhaps it is, but it also makes a decent size operation actually function when you can successfully delegate responsibility, authority, and accountability up and down a management tree. The superior to these two had made a decision, and I was going to respect that. The second reason was that these people were now damaged goods. There was no reinstating them once they had been told they were fired, they were never going to be good employees after going through that trauma. Even if they were right about everything they said, reinstatement still wasn't a possibility.

Now, the irony, of course, is that I suspect now that both were absolutely correct, in everything they said. Unfortunately, though, that still doesn't change anything. It was my responsibility to have a better manager for them, and so their termination was my failure in setting a situation that came to that outcome. By the time it happened there was no putting Humpty Dumpty back together again.

So, when you're about to appeal your firing, keep that in mind. The higher authority would have to not only recognize the mistake of their subordinate, and be willing to correct it with an unbelievably messy reinstatement, but they would then have to admit that the manager was making such serious mistakes as terminating good employees. This would essentially mean that they needed to fire that manager. It's just too many major mental hurdles for a boss to deal with in a day, and you're not going to get your way.

Not to mention, this being politics, people will just lie to your face anyway.

A good friend of mine was fired from this job he had put his heart and soul into, and was fired for the silliest, most inane of reasons. He had a great relationship with the president so he appealed it the next day. The president told him, despite his signature on the termination paperwork, that he agreed with the terminated employee and couldn't understand why his vice president had done this. But, unfortunately, the president couldn't do anything.

Lies, lies, and more lies, of course. This nonprofit president could have snapped his fingers and reinstated this poor fellow, or gotten him another job in politics quite easily. It was just his way of getting out of a tough bind through interesting wordplay and arguments, essentially saying that he, as the boss, was powerless.

Leave gracefully instead, and save the effort to finding the next great opportunity.

You can, despite what intuition might tell you, keep a good relationship with most people from the position. As I said before, many firings are not done by people happy about it or feeling as though it was entirely just. Firings happen for a variety of reasons, and the people involved are distinct from their roles and titles. Besides, everyone has an innate desire to be loved by even their enemies, so unless you want to have an acrimonious relationship with someone, it's not a foregone conclusion.

I went through one firing at the direction of a vice president who told me that if I didn't fire that employee I would be fired as well as my supervisor. So, even though it was unpleasant, there's no reason that you can't maintain a friendship even with those who directly terminate you. I went through a separate, entirely acrimonious firing, and less than a year later we were having drinks, laughing about it, and becoming friends again. It seems like a remote possibility, but with the right personalities, it's not impossible.

This is obviously another good reason to leave gracefully, because politics is a small business and word gets around fast. Keeping a good relationship with everyone, even those who are hurting you, is always a good idea.

And if the place is known for high turnover, realize that and take some satisfaction from knowing the boss's head is likely on the chopping block soon as well. If you're being fired for minor things, or for made-up things, it's just a matter of time before minor problems and made-up things get levied against those firing you.

If you've made a major mistake, however, that's a slightly different situation. Every firing is going to have some ostensible "reason" for the firing, but some are more real than others. If you lie about something, bank on being fired. On a campaign, and even in political organizations, there are so many laws and regulations to run afoul of that sometimes a termination is necessary even though your "wrong" was very low. But if you did something major, like stealing from the campaign, breaking an opponent's yard signs, or talking to reporters without permission, the circumstances are quite different.

First, if a major mistake occurs, you need to ask yourself some questions. Politics can get to you to such a degree that almost anything seems possible. When you're telling everyone that the Republic itself depends on the election of your candidate, or that thousands of babies are going to die tomorrow from your issue being neglected, it's easy to believe your own direct mail and go native. Certain things are understandable, certain things are understandable if you're under pressure or young and immature or worked to the bone and making irrational decisions.

But those rationalizations might excuse the responsibility, but they don't change the result. If you're underpaid and lift a few dollars from the campaign, you're getting fired when you get caught, no matter how desperate your situation. If you destroy yard signs of your opponent, which is a crime, you're getting fired even if you're a teenager who didn't know better. So don't think you can escape the liability for major mistakes, or talk your way out of it. The best solution, almost always, is to tell your boss what you've done and come clean before you get caught. Just lay it out and offer to make things right.

Barring that, if you haven't yet been caught and coming clean won't work, resign and find another position. Finding mistakes made by past employees is never as serious as finding out that someone currently on staff made one. And you don't want to come to work fearful someone will find out, or be blackmailed or pressured by someone who knows your secret. But don't let the mistake go unspoken and then let the media find it out and run it a day before the election, or have an opponent or someone with an axe to grind slip that info to a major donor. Those are, trust me, worse situations than telling your boss from the get-go or resigning and finding another position.

If you can predict an impending termination, though, trust your gut and leave on your own terms. You're unlikely to be so off-base about the office environment and not picking up on clear signs of what's coming. One trick I've used when feeling this way is to ask my boss about future plans and ask them about a project we could work on six months from now. I hesitate to share this trick because I suspect you won't believe how easy and accurate it is: if you're boss fumbles and has odd expressions about the future, you know that a termination is coming unless you can change the situation.

If you know or suspect that it's coming, get everything personal out of your office: your personal files, emails, trinkets, pictures, everything. This won't go unnoticed, but you can give a plain statement that those things were just distracting you and you know that you need to keep focused and meet your goals and not have your mind wander.

I am a bit of a packrat, and after two and a half years at one job, I saw the writing on the wall and had boxes of books and other items I needed to get out in a jiffy. I asked a friend with a van to pull around front, and in the morning I was offloading scores of things into his van, which in hindsight must have been quite a sight to see. As I was pushing a dolly through the company lobby the organization president walked by and didn't say a word. I had the termination hearing later that day, and easily would have lost all those items to their human resources minions had I not absconded with my materials. Now, I should also note that I was the proper owner of all these things and I didn't make off with that which was not properly mine. There's no need to become a thief as you become unemployed.

And again, make backups of all your electronic files and contact lists. At that same job I was good about getting my books and bad about getting my emails, some of which contained personal info, such as my Christmas travel itinerary, a few website passwords, and even sweet notes from a girlfriend, all of which I regretted losing. Make those backups, and store them off-site.

Again, don't copy information or lists that aren't yours to take. And remember that most tech guys can easily note what you copied and whether you copied the girlfriend's love notes or the organization's donor database.

The consequences to getting fired can be overblown as well. Your friends might be shocked and amazed, your parents might be upset, but ultimately life goes on and you probably won't notice much different at all. Count on people at the campaign or organization you left knowing. If you were there a short period, meaning less than one year at an organization or less than three months on a campaign, people will presume from your resume that you were fired. For security clearances and certain graduate school applications, it will come up as well, only as something you need to give proper context and explain.

Make sure to keep a copy of the termination letter and any documentation they give you. If they state a reason written out, even if that isn't the real reason, that's what you're bound to disclose, if you must, later. Whatever you hear from others is nice, and whatever you think they fired you for is one thing, but the written version is binding. Most of the time, what's written will be much nicer to you than the real reasons, so this is a good thing.

A common vague statement is "failure to meet goals" or some variation.

This is a positive thing because it allows you a lot of flexibility when discussing it later. The way you discuss firings with future employers and in job interviews, if it comes up at all, is bound by those written statements. And there are always good neutral ways to discuss it, even so simply as to say that things didn't work out, or that the job wasn't a good fit. Throwing in a short discussion about what you learned from the experience is always good.

Professionals won't ask you, though. They might assume from your resume, or the lack of any references from that job, but the good places won't ask. This is why you always include one friend from that job who can say good things about you, even if they weren't a superior or even in your department. I've often seen people who, even when they weren't asked, offer the information and also a few disparaging comments about that group or campaign.

Both are mistakes: don't mention it unless asked because professionals don't ask in the first place; and never disparage a previous employer.

For starters it makes your current employer consider how you'll speak of them in a few years at your next job interview. And it never creates a positive association. Badmouthing a place that gave you a paycheck just always seems like it's the employee and not the employer who was the real scoundrel. I had people come to me who knew that I had bad experiences at one place I had worked, and they would constantly disparage this place that had wronged me, and I caught myself defending it to them.

If you work at a place, you never want to think it was all a mistake. You want to think that you made a positive contribution during your time there, and when you disparage a place, you make it seem as though it is all-bad, and that badmouthing says a lot more about you than it does about the bad organization or campaign.

Project an optimistic attitude and appreciate the opportunities given, even by tough employers.

In a way, it's like when a girl badmouths a previous boyfriend. One can't help but wonder, then, why that girl dated such a loser and such a miscreant given her many complaints. If that other person was so bad, then by implication one assumes that she is so bad because she was with him. Institutions are the same way, when you badmouth an institution, you're saying that you were there while those things happened, and are guilty by association, in this case association to the same complaints you're now making about it. You are metaphorically throwing mud at yourself.

Avoid the temptation and don't badmouth previous employers, candidates, or groups. And save the gossip for future lunches, not in the interview or in the first few weeks you work a new place.

The right way to talk about a previous employer is with a positive attitude, appreciative of their opportunities to learn good skills, meet good people, and open the door to the bright future you will talk about with your future interviewers. Deal with the past issues by talking about the positive ways they have helped you develop and evolve as a serious worker and politico, and don't fall into the trap of badmouthing anyone or any place. And even if offered the bait to badmouth previous people, stay positive, chipper, and pleasant. Everyone will be happy you did.

If you find yourself fired from two places in a row, it's time to step back and consider how to avoid this situation in the future. It's easy to rationalize one away, but two in a row from different groups is a definite warning flag. At a minimum, after being fired, make sure that you are employed at the next place for a solid year or more, otherwise your resume will look like you're either unemployable or a flake. Hiring managers won't call you because they'll assume you are regularly either getting fired or "better dealing" them constantly.

Chapter 8. Finding Better Jobs and Getting Promoted

To re-emphasize, always keep an updated resume ready. You never know when you'll need one in a hurry—when a perfect opening will come up that you need to react quickly to seize upon.

At any job, the frustrations can lead you to conclude that supervisors are the most foolish people in the world or to rationalize the bad policies by saying that every place has its drawbacks. But the mistake in both situations is not channeling your frustrations into potential self-advancement and promotion.

Frankly, many promotions occur when an employee who was taken for granted is suspected of eyeing other organizations. Similar to how a girlfriend or boyfriend is never more attractive than when they're flirting with someone else, people are more likely to reward to keep what human capital they have than to reward for merit. You can use this to your advantage. Don't make a show about it, and certainly don't tell anyone at work what you're doing, but your confidence will go up and people will notice. Managers tend to have a sixth sense about when this is happening, and tend to offer promotions and pay raises to retain good people in lieu of the heavy costs of losing the employees they value.

One easy way to angle for a promotion, and demonstrate your own laudable ambition, is to run for office yourself. Be aware of local filing deadlines, but the number of votes needed for most local offices is amazingly low. Many college student government offices are more competitive than a local school board race. Check the filing deadlines, and don't run for a position in competition or at odds with the candidate or cause you're working for. There are elected positions within your party in several states, races few ever run for and are easily won. Running for these races and winning makes you immediately relevant to the organization, and is a great stepping stone to a job in politics. A multitude of books cover starting your campaigns from scratch, so I won't cover it here, but it's a good option to get yourself noticed.

And even if you don't decide to run for an office yourself, getting a friend or family member to run can provide a good lateral move to another campaign, giving you a good chance to test your budding skills with another candidate. As well, if the office is uncontested enough, you can often continue volunteering for the campaign and work on both contests.

Many people working in politics or campaigns consider themselves learned and expert enough to become political consultants. They consider their valuable advice, and the great amounts of money spread around campaigns, and realize that they only need a fraction of that money in order to do politics full-time and avoid the hard grunt work that comprises most campaigns and most political groups. Resist this temptation. It's extremely enticing, and you might even find a few clients, but I predict two things will happen: 1) you will experience a great deal of personal poverty, as most people in your situation overrate their own wisdom, skills, and potential client base; and you will also 2) overrate your ability to survive the natural cycles of politics. Everyone needs a consultant, or so it seems, in September and October before a November election, but no one needs one in December after the election, and many campaigns don't hire staff except in the few months before the election.

Even political organizations still follow a very cyclical season tied to election day. They want to be active and educating voters while the voters are paying attention to politics. It might seem that issue groups would want to be active when elections aren't stealing people's attention, but the opposite is the case. Groups and organizations want to be relevant while politics is at fever pitch, and so even non-campaign political jobs are hard to find during the low ebbs.

The cliché to always hit people up for lunch, meeting them for lunch that is and not trying to get them to pay for yours, is also a good way to protect yourself during those low ebbs. Networking lunches are a great way to get a better job and also get a promotion. I never found it easy to fall into this routine, and it always seemed like a chore, but during the lunch I was always glad I did it. You don't need a good excuse. Just go through your list of Facebook friends in the area, your cell phone list, or your Christmas card distribution list, and ask people out to lunch just to catch up. Keep the occasion social and friendly, and don't make it overtly about business.

This can seem overly costly when you're poor, but it's something you have to do in order to stay in the loop. Lunch is an important part of being well-networked within politics.

Also accept any invitation to lunch that comes up. You can find out about gossip, open job positions, and information that is often quite useful. As well, it's the best way to "meet" people in politics and develop friendships. It's rare to have enough time at a political function to really develop a relationship, but a lunch is intimate enough where you feel like you really get to know the other person. It's a meal designed perfectly for politics. Also, if it's someone you're not familiar with or someone is a known epic talker, let them know that you have to leave after an hour no matter what. Having cash on hand to leave it in case of a slow waitress is another good idea, so you don't have to wait and split the check with a long-talker.

Your extended network and these political lunches can also be useful to vet potential job applicants and find out people's strengths and weaknesses. It sounds extremely gossipy to write that, but it's true. If you are involved in the hiring process, you need a way to determine if that odd recent applicant is a known stalker or has a serious, known porn addiction. Is one of your major donors about to go bankrupt? Is another political organization about to receive a million dollar gift and they want to hire someone with your exact skill set? This is where you find these things out. And these lunches are the way to do that, a nice informal way to gossip and find out this information and much more.

Lunches can also provide for positive surprises as well. I went to lunch with a somewhat informal business contact three months into a new job, and he flat out offered me a much more prestigious job in politics, even though he didn't work there anymore. I had no reason to expect this to be the case, but we went through the pleasantries and he said a D.C. magazine had an unposted opening at and that they knew my work and my work ethic and that I'd be great for the position. Again, I didn't feel as though I knew this person that well, but they obviously had a serious need for a good person, and felt like I was the right person for the position.

Go to lunch with other people, you won't regret it.

The secret to the most effective lunches is to do favors for other people. Everyone talks about the things they need, or prattle on about their problems, find ways to solve their problems. And while advice and suggestions are always useful, real help is the major difference. Does a friend in another campaign have a major mailing to get out and you have idle interns? Make sure this works with local and state laws, but if it does, send them over and help out with the mailing.

This is the difference between mediocre political players and real professionals. Professionals get things done and solve problems, and the tourists sit and give their opinion and other useless words.

People have real problems, politics has tough situations, find ways to solve them and you'll develop a level of loyalty from other people that is unmatched. Winning elections is about money, votes and time but politics is about doing favors.

One friend made their mark and started their career by matching volunteers with campaigns that needed them. The statewide Secretary of State wanted college students to wear their t-shirts at conventions, and students wanted the free hotel rooms and food that came with. The campaign was happy and the students were well fed, being a middle man can keep your phone ringing and that wheel is greased through favors.

By talking to people in other organizations, you'll soon appreciate the kind of needs and skill sets other organizations are consistently looking for, and who they can never seem to find. Most organizations want someone who is conversant in fundraising technology, a reliable hard worker, and a known commodity.

So, seeing these needs, start working on your own skills in the needed areas. Make your supply meet the stated demand. Pick up a book on fundraising, try your hand at a fundraising letter, or go on a donor visit and see what it's like. Get involved with what truly "adds value" to the organization or campaign in the most demonstrable way.

Make a list of the skills you know are in high demand, even just a matter of writing an email to yourself. Then identify someone who is well-skilled in that area, and take them to lunch and pick their brain about how to become better skilled in the topic. Almost always there's a basic book or primer to get started on that skill, and something that will enable you to start a discussion with them.

These are the kind of things that hard workers do, the actions taken by people who aren't just moping around collecting a paycheck. And a lot of social climbers can feel as though this is a waste of time, or you watch someone else in the office who goes to all the social parties, follows none of this advice, but seems to be more popular and better accepted than you. First, realize that being publicly seen and widely admired is a skill. But also know that their shallowness toward the job, and their somewhat flippant attitude about the real work being done, is being noticed as well. People can like someone, but still know that they're the wrong person for the job.

And more often than not, good nonprofits, campaigns, parties, and legislative jobs assess promotion, performance, and raises on much more of a merit basis than it seems on the surface. You attend parties and see what you think are the office politics dynamic, but good managers play their cards close to their chest, and you're often guessing the wrong outcomes. Don't assume you're being ignored or that your work isn't seen. It is, and your work will quickly speak for itself.

That reputation for working hard and staying focused will also be noticed by your coworkers and many others. Keep focused and good things will happen.

Chapter 9. Leaving the Job, Getting a New Job

There are a variety of good reasons to leave a job, and, of course, many opportunities will come your way if you follow the advice in this book. A few good indicators of when it's the right time to make a move is when the opportunity is truly better, not just perceived as better. Make sure that you're either getting at least a 10 percent raise through the new job, significant job title improvement, or a serious career change that suits you, and ideally two of those three things. You don't want to make a change in the political world just because it seems like it'll be a better organization or that the department leader will be stronger. In truth, each job has its drawbacks and negatives, and so, despite perceptions, a job is always going to involve a good deal of work.

Many political places, though, have unstated promotion plateaus, where your potential for upward advancement is limited or non-existent. These places are good places to work for a period, but don't hold some false illusion about your potential there, don't make plans on breaking the mold because you ought to make your plans off of what you've observed other people doing. That might seem like very conservative advice, but it's a dangerous thing to hold out for what's never happened before, or rarely happened. And many places abuse their position as a place where you can work on your passions and dangle the expectation of a promotion that will never come. Sit back and ask if you see a realistic chance for you to get promoted, and whether that position will ever open up for you.

A good person to ask is someone who doesn't work with you, who can give you honest feedback. Perhaps this is a boyfriend or a girlfriend, or perhaps it's a friend from college or a mentor, but get that honest feedback and see where you're at and their advice on where you can go from where you're at. Another good indication of your position at an organization is during your annual raise. If you get anything less than five percent as an annual raise, you're losing money from inflation and the organization doesn't really value your work. This is a good indication to start looking elsewhere.

As a former manager, let me tell you how relatively insignificant the staff salaries are in the overall budget. If someone needed a raise, they could get one. But the difficulty is in simply asking for one, just having the temerity to approach your boss with the request for a raise. Another common misconception is that these things come naturally or are the rewards for a long year. Quite the contrary, a place will not give you anything you don't ask for, and won't give anything to you without pressure to do so. Each year you will likely have to ask for a raise at your annual review.

Some places skip or make a mockery of the annual review, which is a mistake as well. You want the feedback and the valuable insight it can provide, and most importantly you want the chance to ask for a raise. Be firm, and even if it has been a mediocre year, ask for 10 percent knowing they might meet you halfway at five. They certainly won't give you more than you ask for, and in asking and observing their reaction, you see how much they really want you. During this review, of course, your supervisor will immediately latch onto the half-dozen perceived mistakes you made during the year as implied reasons not to approve your raise.

And just ignore those comments and give only muted acknowledgment, because it's an act to get you out of the mindset that you're entitled to a raise. But, again, you need to get a raise just to make ends meet. I knew a fellow who worked five years for the same organization and never got a raise, but of course never asked for one. By the time he finally asked for one, they gave it to him, but he was so financially despondent that he had to move away from D.C. anyway; it was too late. Realize your own workplace worth, don't be afraid to ask for a raise when appropriate, and appreciate its usefulness in determining how your employer views your contributions.

If you don't get a raise, or your boss decides to bring up every petty wrong you've committed over the past year, start looking for another position. It's odd how the comfort of miserable places can become compelling. The security of what's known and familiar is a powerful force that prevents a positive move, a weighty personal inertia that precludes you from greener pastures elsewhere. My first job out of college was an entirely bad fit between my manager and I. We didn't gel well, and I always felt as though I was on the verge of being fired.

And yet, when I had another offer and was about to tell my boss about my impending departure, it was difficult. I looked around at the people I knew and whose company I enjoyed; I thought about the projects I still wanted to finish; I thought about the "good work" I thought that I was doing and the work was doing. The pressure to remain where you're at is strong and irrational. The job I left for was made for me, and probably the most rewarding position I've ever had, and even though I was leaving an awful situation, I still felt those pressures to remain.

It's worth remembering the truism that a good manager never changes a bad organization, rather, a bad organization changes a good manager into a bad one. If you're a small cog in a big poorly-run machine, quit beating your head against the wall and hoping that the dawn is about to rise on a new era. More likely than not, nothing will ever change, don't make your life plans on the expectation of unreasonable change.

Poorly run and poorly managed places can seem all the more secure because you've been mentally and emotionally beaten into submission. You won't realize it at the time, but the constant pressure of the workplace environment has an enormous impact upon you, and your attitude reflects that, all the more reason to jump at the opportunity to jump at better opportunities.

Places with bad management and employees who feel this way are also ones that run into a variety of other problems stemming from bad management. Specifically, many organizations that can't motivate their people can't motivate their donors and can't get their board motivated to rustle up the cash to keep paying people. Sadly, this is an all-too-common experience, as well as organizations that refuse to pay people what they're owed or refuse reimbursements banking on you not taking them to small claims court later.

A place with bad management in one area often has many other areas of bad management that's wise to avoid. An old adage is that "personnel is policy," meaning that how you treat your employees, and how your employees act and perform, is the essence of every company. So don't lose the opportunity to move, weighed down by irrational inertia, when there are plenty of problems to leave.

Campaign jobs are also seasonal, and if you get a better job a few weeks before the election, you should try to delay accepting the position until after the election. But no one can blame you for taking it because the day after election day, and sometimes before, you hit the curb. Field staff, especially, are often unneeded when the campaign shifts purely into turnout mode, depending on the budget. Many campaign managers will bristle at me giving you this advice, because they often rely on people who don't have other positions who can take up the slack in those tense final weeks, but if you get a good stable position, take it and don't look back. No one is going to look out for your interest better than you will.

Chapter 10. Leaving Politics/Changing Your Role

When you get into, or are getting into, politics it seems like you are finally "home" and that you'll never leave. You probably have several years of watching politics diligently, working on campaigns, and indulging this passion in many ways so that it feels like you're finally getting paid to work your hobby—that this isn't traditional "work," but really being paid to do what you love. And, unfortunately, everyone else knows this and takes advantage of that fact to the point that many political workers never really get paid enough to live, and will never be paid enough to make a truly stable career in politics.

Politics is a great way to meet some fabulous people, though, and if you have the passion for the profession, it's probably always going to be better to have tried it out than to have always wondered, "what if?" But there does come a point where you should honestly and objectively assess your future.

When you've been working campaigns or for a political outfit for a few years, make a mental list of your successes, the things that you're truly proud of, and relish those moments. And now, ask yourself if you will likely have those same kind of successes in the future. Talk to a friend who doesn't work in politics, a mentor or perhaps a parent, and ask them their advice: whether you are doing well enough to continue in this career or if it might be time to gently ease yourself out.

Quite frankly, if you look around, you'll often struggle to find people who are making careers out of politics. You'll notice many twenty-something's working their fingers to the bone, older people who have made their money elsewhere and don't have to worry about a paycheck, and people who are independently wealthy or trust fund beneficiaries. People in their thirties—people with families—have an extremely tough time staying in politics as a career. How can you save enough for an average wedding, for example, when working on campaign salaries or always dealing with the drama with nonprofits? You can't, and it's not set up to be a career.

It's also very hard on your relationships with other people to stay working within politics. Your time is always gone, you're always broke, you're often stressed, and, fundamentally, you're alienated from friends and family. You're always thinking about work, or drawn into the drama that work undoubtedly becomes. You're certainly not the person you need to be in your relationship, the friend you need to be to others, and the provider you need to be to yourself. Politics is draining personally, emotionally, and spiritually. You start seeing every dissenter as the "other", people who don't donate as part of the problem, and people who don't vote as complicit in the status quo.

Politics can quickly make you a bad person.

Getting out is difficult, you become entirely entrenched in a siege mentality and a lifestyle that revolves around checking the Drudge Report every five minutes as though you impact this collective consciousness of politics. It's an unhealthy fixation on the news cycle, on minor victories that too often are electoral successes that set back the real issues.

Everyone in politics needs to ask themselves what are their first things—what are the things that really matter to them? Politicos have an easy mental defense when they reflexively dismiss the idea of "selling out" to business. But "selling out" is also a means of providing for yourself without massive credit card debt, and providing for a real, serious, stable career and family. And for all the temptation to consider "selling out," one ought to question the real lasting impact of one's political efforts and victories. At the risk of sounding like a cynic, it's too easy to start believing your own direct mail packages, and start overemphasizing your efforts. An iota of understanding of chaos theory will allow you to mentally connect every act your organization does with every bit of good done in the political world, but we both know that's not true.

Be serious, objective, and analytical about your political efforts. Where have you succeeded, where have you failed, and what do you want to do with your life? My moment of true realization on this point was working a job I enjoyed, for a boss I loved, with a decent chance of promotion and decent possibility of organizational growth, but realizing that it was almost equally as likely that in a decade I would be working the exact same job doing the exact same thing, too often involving stuffing envelopes and making a mailing for a drop date deadline by the close of the business mail window. I wanted a family and a career where I was reaching my full potential. Sadly, politics doesn't afford that chance very often, it treats its people as relatively disposable units because there are so many people who want to do it.

It also cultivates this sad element, a combination of depression and low self-worth. You'll hear a lot of people say that they can't do other things, or don't feel as though they could handle the monotony of business. They use these as quasi-psychological reasons to prevent them from changing their situation. They rationalize their troubles as the only option open to them. The truth is that a great deal of what is done in politics is useful in the business world, and your experiences are valuable and demonstrate a great degree of leadership, intelligence, creativity, and courage. Writing direct mail letters helps you write ad copy. Dealing with reporters teaches you how to be a journalist, and you learn almost all the basic principles of marketing on the cheap very quickly on any campaign. Management of people to accomplish a goal is the project management skill anywhere.

For as often as people in politics feel like they would never work in the business world, many people in the business world are very respectful and appreciative of politics.

I've met the best people through politics, and yet the best ones always leave. That's not because they "sold out" or because they didn't have the endurance to live a life of chaos, frustration, and low-pay. During the 2004 Presidential campaign, John Kerry's first wife made a comment to the press that she didn't want to talk about politics anymore because she associated it purely with anger, rage, paranoia, and frustration, and that she was glad to have it in the past and not in her future. That's a telling statement, and not the exception. It's a tough business, and I hope you do good things but then use a good opportunity to build a sustainable life for yourself.

If you take your opportunity to get out, there is still much good you can do as a strong leader in your community. After-school programs that you help out at can easily change lives, and being an honest, ethical political candidate is a sad rarity. You can be that person after saving money (or paying down your debts) and putting roots in a community. Politics is a passion, but it's not a passion that most people can sustain as a career. And if it feels like it is turning into a career, make sure it's serving all your real needs and fulfilling those first things.

Find a job that pays well and has regular hours. And don't think that you don't have skills to offer. Once you get into a good schedule and routine, your work life and work day will pass with ease. Focusing your attention at the workplace will initially be tough, but once you do you'll do great. The skills you learned doing everything last minute and on the cheap will be great in a business environment where they give you reasonable times to finish a project and have the funds allocated to actually accomplish the project without digging through the trash for office supplies.

If you've worked on a campaign, you've started a small business from nothing. After working in politics, you have certainly become a better writer. If you've ever fundraised through the phone, you've learned the essential basics of sales. When you objectively assess your accomplishments on a campaign, it's not hard to see where they can easily fit into a business. Also, most journalists have never worked on a campaign; most high school government teachers haven't either. Perhaps even more shockingly, most college political science professors are spectators to the sport, and have never worked on a campaign.

Your experience sets you apart, and your time working long hours has many great potential outgrowths. Pursue them when the time is right, and find a way to pay your bills, support yourself, build a family, and indulge your passions after taking care of those first things. Come to politics with the independence you need to be the candidate, or to be the major donor who dictates issues, instead of the perpetual low-level staffer who gets overworked and underpaid. As with many other industries, politics is a pyramid scheme where those at the top are doing well, but it's very difficult to work half-way up and pay your debts. Do what works for you, but don't spend decades bleeding for the cause if you can't make your bill payments. By this point you've paid your dues, and you've earned the right to come back to politics later in a position where you can call the shots, and where you can have more of the authority.

Conclusions

Fundamentally adding value to yourself, your resume, and your overall portfolio is what gets you noticed and makes employers want to employ you. Your qualifications are a minimum, but it's quite different for someone to actively desire you, specifically, as an employee. And given the job market, and the fierce competition for political jobs, it behooves you to overthink and overplan for this interaction. You can rise rapidly in politics if you get the right jobs and do well in those positions, and it's a vicious lifestyle. Small mistakes are punished; making the wrong enemies and alienating the right people can have lasting consequences that you never know.

People in politics love to compare themselves to business, and in this regard the comparison shows the difficulty of political success and the ease of business success. People who dislike you may still buy your widget, but in politics people who claim that they like you might never help you or worse, actively work against you behind your back. It's a tough lifestyle, and you need to be within a culture of constant self-improvement to reach your full potential and rise as fast as you should.

Winning a political campaign opens up a world of possibilities, as the role and extent of government is rapidly expanding year by year. Regardless of your philosophical disposition, you will find plenty to keep you busy and occupied once you get your candidate or yourself into office.

You're putting your beliefs and passion into action, but you can't treat it like a hobby anymore. If this is going to be your livelihood, you have to be truly great. As a former employer used to say, you owe it to your beliefs to learn how to win, and to succeed.

Appendices

Appendix A: Political Terms

Direct Mail - the type of mail that solicits for donations to a cause or candidate.

Direct Solicitation - asking for political donations in person

Election Cycle - The period between one election and the next for a particular office. Sometimes this is also considered the period when people are focused on the next election.

FEC - the Federal Elections Commission

Filings - various state and federal filings that many campaigns, nonprofits and other political entities have to submit.

Lists - lists of data of voters, potential voters, donors

Major Donor - the type of identified potential donor who is capable of giving a large gift, as defined by the campaign.

Political Technology - skills that are essential to success in politics

Vendors - people who outsource various functions of the campaign, such as the fundraising vendor, or specifically the direct mail vendor. There are vendors for anything and everything a campaign could want.

Voter Database - each campaign's database of voter information

Voter Vault - the RNC's database of voter information, controlled by each state party.

Appendix B: Great Books Relevant to Politics

Dedication and Leadership by Douglas Hyde

This book is written by a former Communist turned Christian who illustrates the enormously effective organizing tactics of the Communists.

Influence: The Science of Persuasion by Robert Cialdini

All politics is persuasion and marketing, either to voters, donors or volunteers. This book gives one a startling look inside the mind and persuasive techniques in a very readable way. Becoming more persuasive will make you much more effective within politics.

Politics the Wellstone Way by Bill Lofy

Writing how to start and run issue campaigns, as well as general rules within politics, this training primer which is part of the Camp Wellstone political action training, is an excellent read.

Road to CEO by Sharon Velos

Velos writes about the ways individuals can refine and polish themselves to become truly great, worthy of promotion and appealing to others.

Rules for Radicals by Saul Alinsky

A classic that has recently become more well-known, Alinsky's classic primer on political tactics is very amoral and unethical, but focused on results. While it's not a way to conduct politics, it's an essential read to understand effectiveness and tactics that work.

Ogilvy on Advertising by David Ogilvy

Similar to the relevance of Cialdini's "Influence", Ogilvy on Advertising illustrates the principles behind basic visual marketing. For the creation of literature and marketing materials on a small campaign or non-profit that can't afford pricey graphic designers, this book is a must-read.

Appendix C: Political Technology Training Outfits

American Majority (right)

Camp Wellstone (left)

Center for Progressive Leadership (left)

The Leadership Institute (right)

Progressive Majority (left)

State Parties, Democrat and Republican

American University Campaign Management Institute (non-partisan)

American University Lobbying Institute (non-partisan)

George Washington University Applied Politics Seminars (non-partisan)

University of Akron (non-partisan)

Unions (left)

Young People For (left)

(note: there are many more, this is but a small list to get you started)

Appendix D: Types of Jobs

Legislative/Politician Offices

These are jobs with elected officials, either assisting with the passing of laws or with constituent work, helping citizens in your district with problems typically involving the government.

> Perceived sexy: 8
> Actual sexy: 6
> Difficulty to get: 8
> Difficulty to keep: 6
> Pay: 6

Campaigns

Campaign work is thrilling, but comes at the cost of low-pay and long hours. Most people do campaign work for a certain period of their life and then move on to other areas that are more stable and secure.

> Perceived sexy: 9
> Actual sexy: 3
> Difficulty to get: 5
> Difficulty to keep: 8
> Pay: 1

Non-profits/NGOs/501(c)3s

Nonprofits have a mixed record because so many are poorly-run, and yet many do great work. They can be stable, but can be stable at a low-level of performance. You really have to search for the right place, or be willing to make transfers to places that will work for you to avoid getting stuck in a dead-end job in the nonprofit world.

> Perceived sexy: 4
> Actual sexy: 8
> Difficulty to get: 3
> Difficulty to keep: 9
> Pay: 5

Government

Working within the government isn't perceived to be as worthy as other outlets, but these positions often wield a tremendous amount of behind-the-scenes power and influence that can do great things for your cause. The perception of bureaucrats as lazy and bored is often true, but as a motivated and focused person you can easily stand out in that environment.

> Perceived sexy: 3
>
> Actual sexy: 5
>
> Difficulty to get: 7
>
> Difficulty to keep: 2
>
> Pay: 9

Journalism/Writing

The media is an increasingly tough market to break into because of the great changes the industry is going through right now. If you want to enter this market, make your writing strong and your sources plentiful and varied. You can do great things by reporting and telling stories that often get ignored, but you may have a hard time paying your bills if you want to make it a full-time gig.

> Perceived sexy: 6
>
> Actual sexy: 5
>
> Difficulty to get: 5
>
> Difficulty to keep: 4
>
> Pay: 2

Major Donors/Handlers

Most are unaware these jobs even exist, and they're tough to come by. Major donors and people who are wealthy enough to be active in many groups, however, need someone to be their "point person" for their political involvement. If you can build up the trust of someone of wealth, whom you likely already know and have contact with, you can coordinate their political involvement and donations in a way that gives you job stability and gives them an activist on call, a great situation for everyone.

> Perceived sexy: 4
>
> Actual sexy: 6
>
> Difficulty to get: 9
>
> Difficulty to keep: 4
>
> Pay: 8

Appendix E: Potential Starting Points

Campaign Intern

Call the state party and find out who the most competitive seats in your area are, and then call that campaign and say you want to help out today. Go down to the office and start volunteering, most likely by licking envelopes and making phone calls.

Government Intern

Apply for an internship in a government office, often unpaid but sometimes not. Even a two-month internship can demonstrate that you are a reliable person whom they like and enjoy having around. That can lead them to offer you an unannounced position or a position shortly opening, and help steer you to it by telling the hiring manager to pick you.

Journalism Intern

You must have a portfolio of some kind to get started, so start writing for a local paper or a somewhat prominent blog. Keep a clipping of your best work, and try to write original content that you do actual reporting for. Build up a file of 6-12 really solid pieces that you're proud of, and then find someone who can be critical and give you several ways to improve your portfolio. Call up the section editor for a paper you want to write for, and tell them you'll write something "on spec" for "no kill fee" meaning that there's no penalty for them if they decide not to run the article. Then, do a great job on those initial articles and become a regular with that editor. Once you can get 'in' there, and demonstrate your ability to write, ask your editor to keep an ear out for any openings. In time, they'll find a place for you if your writing is good.

Legislative Office Intern

Definitely the best bet is to start here as the intern and work your way up. Some legislative staffers think interns are a waste of their time, and so they may not care enough to actually call you back. This happened to me once so I called every day for six weeks about an internship, which they eventually gave to me as a college freshman, likely just so I wouldn't call anymore. Many staffers, though, like having interns, even if only to make themselves feel more important. And truth be told, there are plenty of political science majors who take these positions and sneer at them, or treat them lightly, but demonstrating a hard work ethic and a positive attitude will go far. One thing that often gets overlooked are tours in the state capital or the national capitol. And this is a huge staff mistake. Tours are a constituent's primary interaction with an office, and each one of those people knows who your candidate is and votes, which puts them in the most precious box of electoral calculus: the reliable voter. So make the tour great, read up on the history of the building you give tours on, ask for permission to lead the constituent tours, the staff will think you're crazy, but you're crazy like a fox. If you give great tours and excel at this job, which I can confidently say you will based on how lazy most staffers are about it, you will make a great impression on management. And if you don't give tours, or that doesn't work out, find one project or item that you can really excel at. I got a job offer once because I was amazing at constituent mail, and had to be told by the Chief of Staff in a Senate office that my letters were getting noticed too much, and that as an intern I was way overstepping the bounds by asking for casework. That's the kind of "problem" that leads to a job offer, where you're doing too much work and take your roles very seriously.

Major Donor Staff

These jobs are extremely hard to come by, you want to get to know a major donor and impress them to the point where they want to keep you on staff for them. The difficulty is that these people can also command people who have a longer history in politics than you to take these jobs because they're seen as such a safe bet. So, have serious skills that are well-demonstrated, and find a major donor to start a relationship and friendship with where they know and understand your skills. When that happens, in time, they'll create a job for you, but you can't ask them for it or else they'll see you as desiring a handout, which they won't want to give you.

Non-Profit Intern

Almost every non-profit is short-handed, so go in and say that you want to help out. Do your best, put your heart into even the trivial details, and be continually value-added and they'll see and appreciate your value. Don't let them continue to use you for free help, however, and demonstrate that you want paid work to continue. They'll either find the money to pay you or they won't, but most likely they will if they see you as value-added, especially if you have fundraising skills.

Appendix F: Finding a Job Electronically

Your career center and various people who haven't really looked for a job in a decade and likely have never tried to find a job in politics have very outdated ideas about how to get one. You can sign up on every job bank and be the perfect applicant, and never get an interview. This chart is a quick way to consider the effort involved in the various types of job prospecting, and the response rate of potential employers who will return your interest with at least an interview.

Effort / Response Rate

Job Banks:	2 / 5%
Emails:	6 / 15%
Phone Calls:	6 / 20%
Career Counselors:	3 / 15%
References:	4 / 25%
Former Employers:	4 / 40%

As you can see, I would suggest that your references and former employers are your best bet. And that if you have to start from scratch, go with phone calls over email and job banks, you'll have a better return when you're talking to a live person on the phone, when you're an unknown person to them, it's just too easy to delete your email or ignore your voicemail, get a live person and ask them for help.

Appendix G: Typical Political Positions and Titles

The structure of a typical Capitol Hill office

Politician/Elected Representative: votes, speaks, raises money
Chief of Staff (CoS): Oversees the office
Legislative Director (LD):Directs Legislative Focus
Legislative Assistant (LA): handles issues, attends hearings
Legislative Correspondent (LC): handles constituent issues
Scheduler
Staff Assistant SA: answers phones, does a lot of the grunt work
Intern: typically helps with phones and mail

The structure of a typical campaign office

Candidate: speaks, meets and raises money
Campaign Manager
Various directors
   -field: brings in volunteers and votes
   -fundraising: brings in money
   -media: gets notice with local media
   -volunteers: coordinates the volunteers
Field Staff: interacts with volunteers, activists
Interns: can vary by campaign and by the intern

The structure of a typical nonprofit

Board of Directors: reviews an annual report four times a year
President: fundraiser
Executive Director: runs the organization
Vice President: runs their division
Department Director: runs their department, typically the hiring manager
Entry-level staff: does the work within the department
Intern: typically assists the entry-level staff

Appendix H: Budgets and Staff Sizes of Various Campaigns and Nonprofits

Campaigns

> Mike Pence for Re-Election (Indiana 2008)
> > Spent: $1.6 million – Opponent spent: $25,000
>
> Gary Peters for House (Michigan 2008)
> > Spent: $2.5 million – Opponent spent: $4.1 million
>
> Thune for Senate (South Dakota 2006)
> > Spent: $15 million – Opponent spent: $21 million
>
> Obama for Senate (Illinois 2004)
> > Spent: $14.5 million – Opponent spent: $2.6 million

From these few examples a few things should be obvious: Senate campaigns are often more expensive, House races can spend a lot of money even when the races aren't competitive, and that money isn't always the predictor of success.

Staffing questions are made more difficult because no campaign will pay what they could otherwise get from a volunteer. Money is so precious and hard to come by, that it's rare to find a campaign that's generous with pay or with staff sizes. Some campaigns operate as a kind of ghost ship of staff as well, financed through fundraising consultants and active through media and mail houses, never having more than a skeleton crew to be the official campaign. For as often as candidates will claim they all run a "grassroots" operation, most don't.

Nonprofits and campaign organizations

> National Rifle Association (NRA)
> > 4 million members – 205 million budget (2004)
>
> Heritage Foundation
> > 59 million budget (2009)
>
> Planned Parenthood
> > 850 locations – 1 billion budget (2007)

These are huge non-profits, definitely some of the largest in the country. Their budgets range so greatly because the type of work they do is almost limitless. Almost all groups, though, have a core mission and core constituency that they serve. In some cases that's the donors to the organization, in other instances it's the paid membership or the chapters that the group works with. Planned Parenthood, for instance, has donors and has members, but its primary constituency are the 850 clinics nationwide that they are affiliated with. Similarly, other nonprofits will have a variety of ways to get involved, but will likely focus their efforts and attention on a select group of people to focus upon.

As to staff size, a good rule of thumb is that there are between 6-10 staff people per million dollars the organization spends. That's a ballpark number to start from, since many nonprofits spend a lot on consultants or on programmatic work that doesn't involve staff.

Appendix I: Interview Questions You Should be Ready for

Who is your favorite political philosopher?

Did you vote for the candidate in the last election? In the last off-year election?

Do you always support the candidate's political party?

What are your top three political issues?

What's your favorite part about politics?

What's your favorite political movie?

Who is your favorite president?

Why do you want this job?

How long do you plan on working here?

How long do you think is a good commitment for a job like this?

What's your favorite political moment?

Who is your favorite columnist and/or publication?

What skills do you bring to the organization?

How well do you know one of your references?

What was your first campaign?

What got you into politics?

What are all the campaigns you've worked on?

What do you think about the last political scandal?

Where do you see yourself in five years?

What will you do after this job?

When interviews ask these questions, they're looking for solid answers. They want you to be calm, straightforward and honest. They don't want ridiculous answers. A ridiculous friend of mine asks bizarre questions just to "trip people up and get honest answers" but most interviews are entirely plain. They want to see that you look nice, are presentable and normal. If you have the interview, you're being considered for the job. You want to project confidence and competence.

Therefore there's no "right" answer to these questions and you can definitely come off too polished and too smooth. Say them aloud and your answers a few times each before you go, and you'll be calm, conversational, and well put-together.

Another quick note is to avoid the temptation to "name-drop" people you barely know. Be honest with the interviewer, so many people claim to "know" someone mentioned, and it quickly gets obnoxious when it's clear you've just heard their name. Someone you "know" should be someone you've gone to lunch with one-on-one, or could in the future.

There's no penalty for saying that you might know someone through another friend, but that you've just heard of them. Honesty here is more important than being seen as the best connected person. Don't lie about who you know, because the interviewer will likely ask that mutual friend, and that could easily harm you.

Appendix J: How Most People Spend Their Time and Why They Get Fired

      60% putting out fires (office politics, drama, nonsense)

      10% fun stuff (events, speeches, rallies, media)

      30% tedious projects (mailings, dealing with vendors, lists, data)

Effective time management in an organization depends on good planning, and controlling your time. A good example is the way in which email can consume your day if you don't leave it, as it will tempt you to reply to every incoming message as it comes in. A wise way to handle tasks and issues like this, is to remove every distraction to the central thing you're working on, meaning to close your email, end distracting conversations and isolate yourself so you can focus on the task at hand.

There are many very enjoyable things to do in politics, but by definition most people enjoy doing those things. If you want to stand out, be the one who will do the tough tasks and the thankless ones, and get yourself disciplined to do those things by removing your distractions. The internet can be an enormous distraction, so turn it off. If your phone is stealing your time, put it on silent. Do what it takes to use your time effectively.

Reasonable Estimates as to the Reasons Why People Get Fired or are Asked to Leave in Politics

      35% - Office politics

      25% - Poor work performance

      20% - Money runs out

      15% - Drama/relationships

      5% - Random/unknown

Appendix K: Ten Skills Need in Politics and Ten Great Ways to be a Great Employee

1. Telemarketing
2. Lists and data management
3. Volunteer recruitment
4. Social events/party planner
5. Working with college students
6. Staying organized, following up on old tasks
7. Managing a small team to do volunteer projects
8. Photography
9. Basic website issues
10. Writing

This is by no means an exhaustive list, but it's a good starting point for skills you may already have in other forms, and are easily adaptable to a campaign's needs.

1. Always do whatever you're told by your supervisor within reason, and do it exactly how they wanted it, on time, without mistakes.

2. Keep a smile and a positive attitude with everyone as much as you can, save your complaints and problems for your boss.

3. Keep a road atlas in your trunk for when the GPS fails.

4. Keep your campaign/organization's literature in your trunk and leave it in new places, or wherever you go.

5. Carry a backup car charger for the candidate's cell phone type wherever you go.

6. Arrive to events early. And when you get there early, call anyone who is known to be late to things and see if they're going to be late. If they are, it eases the tension to just say "they're running behind and will be here in a few" instead of wondering where those people are.

7. Keep a six-pack of water bottles in your trunk.

8. When you order out for food, do anything but pizza. Everyone does pizza, and people get sick of it. Do sandwiches or subs or Chinese.

9. Slightly overorder food and don't underorder. Give the extras to the interns or the entry-level staff, they'll never forget this.

10. Go to CVS and buy cheap thank you notes, and keep a stack of stamps. Send anyone who helps you a thank you note. Let others borrow some when they see you doing this and want to do the same.

Appendix L: Assessing a Race and a Community, What You can Do

1. Start by looking at historical turnout rates (the election return data)

> One looks at reelection rates and incumbency protection rates to determine how "weak" a race is, by seeing if the incumbent is poorly performing in previous races that are similar to the next election cycle you plan to challenge them in.
>
> **Congress** – rarely competitive, around 95% incumbency re-election
> **Senate** – more competitive, around 60% incumbency re-election
> **Mayor** – varies widely, but assume that a majority are easily re-elected.
>
> Easy re-election is a reflection of having a re-election team already in place, good name identification with the voters, and an existing relationship with major donors. All of these things can be overcome, but when the clock's running having these things in place often puts the current officeholder in a much better position.
>
> The wrong implication is that your guy is likely to lose, just based on the numbers. That isn't the lesson at all, though it often proves true. What it means is that in order to win you need a serious grassroots strategy, and a way to overcome these obstacles.

2. If there's no competitive race immediately apparent, consider doing a different type of political action in **activating a community**

> Several options here include helping a good group develop its fundraising, lists and membership or helping a group coordinate their electoral operations in various ways. Many good-sized groups, and almost all smaller ones, are in a startling state of disorganization and often quite inactive. A strong push from you with skill, talent and focused energy can make a great impact. Ensuring they have the fundraising systems to effectively continue the effective action you have gotten them to do, then, is a self-perpetuating action that activates the community.

3. You want to spend your effort on a group worth your time, though, and so here are a few ways to assess and determine what is a good and active organization Every group will say that they're enormously busy, but there are a few good objective ways to assess that claim.

Checklist for an Active Organization

Every group ought to be recruiting volunteers and taking action in the real world. A group that doesn't recruit volunteers is wasting money and time, and any group that doesn't do real-world outreach and impact the community exists only on paper.

There are plenty of groups that are seen as successful that lack either volunteer recruitment or action, but they are tough places to work for, so figure this out soon. Some places call "outreach" their "field work" or sometimes generically "programming."

Volunteers

a. Do they have ready volunteer projects?

b. Do they have other volunteers your age?

c. Is there a staff person assigned to help and assist with volunteers?

d. Do they have targeted places where they can find new volunteers?

Outreach

a. Do they have a messy mailroom? This is a good thing, as it shows they're doing mailings to the community.

b. Do they have a phone bank or series of phones at a desk for volunteers to come in and make calls? This shows they have a way to reach out to the community.

c. Active places will often have stacks of "white mail", which are the returned bad addresses from a mailing, any decent-sized mailing will have hundreds of these letters lying around.

Appendix M: Major Politicos and How They Got Their Start

The nature of politics is the element of change, and the number of people involved. And though things are always changing, and there are a lot of people involved, success starts somewhere. Those who are at the top of the field are those who have been able to survive and weather the storms for many years. As a consequence of those factors, the entry points for the major players today are not necessarily directly comparable to your own, as none of the major players started by helping on a candidate's website in 1960, for example. But as general examples, and as paths to follow, they offer certain lessons. They're also good names to know. These are people who are not elected but, as consultants, pundits, and interest group leaders, are relevant to your future political career.

Roger Ailes - Republican

> As a television producer, he got into a discussion with a visiting candidate, Richard Nixon, who remembered him and later asked him to serve as his own television director.

Lee Atwater - Republican

> Active in student government, Atwater then started working on gubernatorial and senate campaigns.

David Axelrod - Democrat

> Helping out with local politics as a kid, Axelrod became a journalist and eventually left to work as the communications director of a senate race.

Paul Begala - Democrat

> Earned a law degree from the University of Texas, taught law there, and then left for Bill Clinton's Presidential campaign in 1992.

Morton Blackwell - Republican

> Started in the College Republicans and rose to become its executive director, a position that lead him to run Reagan's 1980 youth effort.

James Carville - Democrat

> First getting a law degree and active in other business pursuits, Carville started by working with small local campaigns before becoming a consultant to President Clinton in 1992.

Ann Coulter - Republican

> Active in conservative campus journalism as an undergrad.

Robert Gibbs - Democrat

> Started as an intern in a congressional office.

Mary Matalin - Republican

> Started on a campaign for U.S. Senate.

Dick Morris - Independent

> Active in student government, Morris then went to work with local races and state assembly races in New York.

Markos Moulitsas - Democrat

> Working as a precinct captain at a young age, went to college and refined his writing, starting the DailyKos blog after graduating.

Terry Nelson - Republican

> Managed a congressional campaign in college, and then went as a field representative for the National Republican Congressional Committee.

Peggy Noonan - Republican

> Worked as a journalist at CBS, under Dan Rather, before eventually becoming a speechwriter for Reagan.

Grover Norquist - Republican

> Volunteered on campaigns as a teenager, and was active in center-right politics in college.

David Plouffe - Democrat

> Started working on a senator's re-election campaign.

John Podesta - Democrat

> Got a law degree and started working in a government agency.

Bob Shrum - Democrat

> Started as a speechwriter for the mayor of New York City.

George Stephanopolous - Democrat

> Started as a legislative assistant in a Congressional office.

Joe Trippi - Democrat

> Started in local campaigns around San Jose, CA.

Some of these major politicos were active in politics in college, making their initial contacts by bringing in speakers, attending events, volunteering at events, etc.

Once, the college partisan group at my college asked for volunteers for a political function that night. It turned out to be a political fundraiser. Not only were we able to attend the event for free, but we were able to be seen in front of politicos and their handlers, the kind of people who would later be hiring managers, just to watch a door and serve food for two hours. The small opportunities like this are plentiful if one looks for them.

There are quite a few familiar names who took different paths, but they often have strong family connections. Consultants like **Harold Ickes** have fathers who were cabinet secretaries, reporters like **Anderson Cooper** are within the Vanderbilt family fortune. Even **Cokie Roberts** is the daughter of the former House Majority Leader. Politics is often a family business, and many of those at the top are there due to connections you likely lack. There is a very definite and unspoken political class, and the backgrounds of those at the top are not always easy to directly follow.

About Ben Wetmore

Ben Wetmore received a degree in political science and history from American University where he studied interest groups. Wetmore has worked for a variety of non-profits and has provided organizational consulting to over 20 groups, foundations, companies, and organizations. Wetmore has trained over 2000 activists in workshops on political organization techniques and helped to start 120 campus publications across the country. He has worked in several states as an administrative assistant, a nonprofit executive director, a campaign manager for a U.S. Senate race, a department head, a nonprofit president, and the director of outreach for a statewide political organizing group, all within the last six years. Living now in New Orleans, he attends the Holy Name of Jesus Church. He's currently working on a law degree.

Made in the USA
San Bernardino, CA
24 November 2012